SCOTTISH ANCESTORS

Life in the Braes of Scotland

1740 – 1876

SCOTTISH ANCESTORS

Life in the Braes of Scotland

1740 – 1876

Jill Tompkins Bailey

Published 2013
By Jill Tompkins Bailey
Berkswell, UK

ISBN 978 0 9927866 0 1

Printed by UKBookprinting, UK.

ACKNOWLEDGEMENTS
The genealogical studies of our family's Scottish ancestors done by Bill Parsons and Jean Hay form the basis for this story. Much of the information about Glenisla came from David Grewer's book, The Story of Glenisla, which is no longer in print. Also valuable was Dr John McKenzie's Pigeon Holes of Memory edited by his great grand daughter Christina Byam Shaw. Many photos used are stored at the Angus Arcives ,Cultural Services department in Forfar.

Sketches by A.J. Bill Bailey.

CONTENTS

Introduction - the fascination of ancestors

Introduction

The Fascination of Ancestors

This is an account of four generations of Scots and how it was that the fourth generation left the Highlands for life in the New World. These people were not in a class which left any written records other than the skeleton outline of their lives as recorded in their births, deaths, marriages and later, census papers. To fill out their experiences I have used various sources which were written at the relevant times and places. It is written particularly for those people who, like our family, have grown up in the New World and have begun to ponder what the lives of their ancestors were really like.

In the twenty first century descendants of Scottish immigrants visiting the land of their ancestors sweep in to Lintrathen and Glenisla along smooth macadam roads. These roads scarcely seem to rise; the pasturelands roll up to smooth heather clad hills with patches of serried rows of Sitka spruce familiar as the commercial pine plantations seen in their far off homelands in Australasia or the Americas. At the level of the grey stone Glenisla church cattle graze on good green pasture and above them large healthy black legged sheep graze, although the predominant vegetation is the purple heather where grouse are nurtured for the formal autumn shoots[1].

---

[1] These grouse shoots begin on the famous August 12th and continue through autumn in to winter. Grouse is an indigenous bird to Britain (unlike pheasant and woodcock) and is not found anywhere else in the world.

This area was once covered by the vast Caledonian forest; at this level, 300 to 500 feet above the sea, the woodland would have been a broad-leafed deciduous forest of oak with birch and alder. Higher than this were pinewoods with birch while above 2000 feet wind and altitude would defeat the trees. During the middle ages these forests were cut down until in the 15th century the Scots Parliament became alarmed enough to pass legislation to limit tree cutting. In the eighteenth century there were still enough trees in Glenisla to provide cover for the cattle thieves. And higher still at Invercauld, which is now for the most part a treeless deer forest, members of the Farquharson family in 1769 were recorded as felling for sale 800 Caledonian pines of 200 years standing.

Eighteenth century travellers to the Highlands were not enamoured - "The eye penetrates far among them [the Highland hills], and sees more particularly their stupendous bulk, frightful irregularity, and horrid gloom, made yet more sombrous by the shades and faint reflections they communicate one to another." And later the same traveller describes a range of mountains as "a dismal brown drawing upon a dirty purple, and most of all disagreeable when the heath is in bloom....the huge naked rocks, being just above the heath, produce the disagreeable impression of a scabbed head."[2] And later in the 18th century Samuel Johnson visiting the Highlands in 1773 wrote "What is not heath is nakedness, a little diversified by now and then a stream rushing down from the steep. An eye accustomed to flowing pastures and waving harvests [of England] is astonished and repelled by this wide extent of

---

Grouse shooting provides an income to land owners
[2] Letters from a Gentleman in the North of Scotland....Edward |Burt 1720 Wilderness

hopeless sterility."

It was not until Sir Walter Scott romanticised the area in his prolific writings that it began to gain the popularity it now has as an area of great beauty -

> "The wanderer's eye could barely view
> The summer heaven's delicious blue;
> So wondrous wild, the whole might seem
> The scenery of a wondrous dream."[3]

Hopefully Andrew Duncan saw his surroundings in this more romantic light when he proposed marriage to Janet Gray in the autumn of 1740. The glen in which they lived had no carriage way in or out of it. Those who left the glen would likely take a narrow pitted path south west towards Alyth and included a hill which could become impassable in winter. It was secluded, bypassed by the military roads of General Wade which went up from Blairgowrie to Braemar. Beside the turbulent river Isla was the old stone church and across the road an inn offering a rough bed for the traveller.

Groups of stone dwellings with roughly thatched roofs were scattered on the surrounding slopes, with small vegetable patches and some rowan trees laden with red berries and the ash just turning into its brilliant yellow foliage beside them. Around these low slung buildings were patchworks of strips for plough, empty now, although it is possible the bad weather of 1740 may have led to some oats not having dried enough to harvest even that late in the year. The small farm animals - kye (the black cattle), ponies and white sheep which were around would have been foraging out what grass they could still find on the unfenced slopes. There were patches of birch and oak and boggy areas leading down to the tributaries of the river Isla held russet coloured marsh grasses, while the Grampian hills rose ever higher behind.

---

[3] verse XII The Lady of the Lake, Sir Walter Scott.

TIMELINE   GLENISLA

1720   John Storrier m Margaret Lindsay (2)

1730

1740   Andrew Duncan m Janet Gray(6)
                   Andrew McKenzie m   Elizabeth Lamond (5)
1750   Charles Grewer m Isobel Clark (5)

1760

1770   Andrew Storrier m Margaret Grewer (5)
                William McKenzie m Margaret Barnet (7)

1780

1790   Elspeth Storrier m John Duncan (10)

1800
                    David Storrier m Janet McKenzie (8)
1810   b.Craigneity Glenisla d Lintrathen

1820

1830   Charles Duncan m Margaret Farquharson(9)
                b Craighead Glenisla d Lintrathen
1840

1850   John Storrier   m   Jane Duncan (6)
                b Sturt Glenisla d Timaru NZ
Bracketed numbers = known number of children.

In 1720 the Storrier family were recorded as Storar.
Andrew Storrier and Margaret Grewer, were the grandparents of
John Storrier and the great grandparents of Jane Duncan. John and
Jane Storrier nee Duncan were the emigrants who began the now
extensive New Zealand branch of this family.
See" A Highland Heritage" by Jean Hay for more detail on the
Farquharsons.

10

TIMELINE   LINTRATHEN

1720

1730   James Farquharson m Maron Lindsay (1)

1740   James Farquharson m Elspet Lowe (1)

1750

1760   Robert Farquharson m Jean Stormonth (2)

1770

1780

1890

1800   Robert Farquharson m Jean Low (2)

1810

1820

1830   Charles Duncan m Margaret Farquharson(9)

1840

1850   John Storrier m Jane Duncan (6)

John and Jane Storrier emigrated to New Zealand in 1876. Their
ancestors had lived in the neighboring parishes of Glenisla and
Lintrathen in Forfarshire for generations.
The Farquharson Line can be traced back to Finlay
Shaw/Farquharson, also known as Finla Mor as he was a large, very
strong man. He was born north of Lintrathen at Invercauld about
1487.

Part 1
MID EIGHTEENTH CENTURY LIFE IN FORFARSHIRE

A cottage in Forfarshire photographed probably early 20th century (with a new addition on the side) photo Angus Council Cultural Services.

Weddings, The Kirk, the home of the agricultural labourer, farming, Jacobites in the Braes, the aftermath of the "45"and the silent clearances, funerals and wakes.....

The Immigrants' Great Grandparents:

Andrew Duncan who married Janet Gray in **1740**
John McKenzie who married Elizabeth Lamond in **1746**
Andrew Storrier who married Margaret Grewer in **1773**
Robert Farquharson who married Jean Stormouth abt **1770**

Chapter 1

A Wedding in the Braes - 1740

Come all ye jolly shepherds
That whistle through the glen,
I'll tell ye of a secret
That courtiers dinna ken:
What is the greatest bliss
That the tongue o' man can name
Tis to woo a bonny lassie
When the kye [cows] comes hame…
'Tween the gloamin' an' the mirk
When the kye comes hame.

See yonder pawkie shepherd
That lingers on the hill,
His ewes in the fauld
An his lambs are lying still;
Yet he downa gang to bed,
For his heart is in a flame,
To meet his bonnie lassie
When the kye comes hame
When the kye…… [4]

It was December of 1740 when Andrew Duncan and Janet Gray were "legally proclaimed" to be married in the Parish of

---

[4] Recorded by James Hogg the "Ettrick Shepherd" at the end of the 18thcentruy.

Glenisla in   Forfarshire. The Proclamation , if called thrice on one day cost them three scots pounds, or just eighteen shillings if made on three successive Sundays. Wedding festivities usually took a week, a welcome diversion in the cold dark winter days when little outdoor activity was possible and hours were spent inside crofts heated only by smoky peat fires. The winters were long "the frosts are generally set in by the end of August and the winters are commonly very severe......it is often the latter end of March or beginning of April before the seed time is begun." [5] It was this prolonged period of hibernation each year that helped form the impression with outsiders that these high country folk were "not indeed so industrious as could be desired". [6]

The first activity in the wedding ceremony   was the contract night when the names were handed in for proclamation. Later friends immersed the feet of the couple in a tub   of water, soap, soot and other unseemly ingredients from which they struggled to get free. Next was the buying of the braws, braws being one's best apparel. During the following week Janet's "flittin" had to be taken to her new home. This "flittin" will have been prepared by Janet and her mother and included the "lint tykin" of linen, blankets, coverlets ; articles such as a wheel and reel for spinning, the rock of the wheel already being covered in lint ready for spinning. The wedding gifts too had to be taken across to Janet's new home; these were of a practical nature - fowls, cheese, butter, eggs, hams and whisky or blankets, cloth, wool, lint and household furniture might also be given. All this had to be taken over the rough tracks there being no roads in the region. Often contained in wooden chests

[5] Statistical Accounts of Scotland. Account of 1791-99 vol 6 County of Forfar, Glenisla.p.391
[6] ibid p.392

these were attached to poles tied to a pony the ends trailing over the ground. Anyone met on the journey had to pause and have a drink to the bride's health.

On the morning of the wedding day, that is the twenty third of December 1740, Andrew's friends and family assembled where he lived while those invited by Janet went to her place. There they ate their respective wedding breakfasts - milk, porridge, mountains of bannocks (round , thick, flattish cakes of oatmeal made of the girdle), heaps of butter and huge lumps of cheese. Thus replenished they drank to Janet and Andrew's health. Andrew then selected a few of his friends to fetch Janet to church, which was known as the "send". On arrival at the church the ceremony took place after which, preceded by pipers, everyone set out for the newly established home.

Andrew and Janet Duncan were to live at Craighead, a couple of miles North of the Kirkton along a rough hill track. Nearing the destination this became a race, for the first to arrive would be awarded a bottle of whisky. Since the excrement pile for people and animals alike lay in front of the house it was not unknown for the runners in their excitement to fall into this midden. There was also a saying used when it was felt that the bride had made an unfortunate choice in her husband: "she was lookin'at the moon and lickit the midden". There is nothing to suggest however that Janet had cause to regret her marriage to Andrew.

Crossing the threshold a large cake (oaten of course) was broken over Janet's head, the pieces eagerly gathered up by the guests. As the croft was too small to accommodate all the guests the barn was swept out and a long trestle table prepared for the feast. This would be a broth swimming with fat, legs of mutton and fat hens, served with melted butter, curds and cream. There may not have been much cream for Andrew and Janet's wedding because 1740 was one of the few years in the eighteenth century when food was short. After drinks and speech making the barn was cleared for dancing to the music of a fiddler, the first dance being for the newly weds, the next for the young unmarried then the dancing would be for everyone.

To complete the ceremony there was the "kirkin" when close family members accompanied the newly weds to church on the following Sunday. This was the last Sunday in December of 1740, and the service was taken by the same minister who married them, the Reverend William Arthur. Mr Arthur was recently come to Glenisla following the deposition on the seventeenth of April of the Rev James Mitchell .The latter had been "deposed for his scandalous and immoral behavior".[7] Tantalizingly we don't know what exactly this behavior was but we do know that the minister himself blamed his dismissal on the personal animosity of a branch of the Ogilvy family who lived just down the river Isla at Eastmiln.

The Rev. Mitchells side of the story went as follows: Thomas Ogilvy was styled a Laird and had married Isobel McKenzie in 1720, probably a local girl as there were many McKenzies in Glenisla. They had five boys and two girls, and these boys being in their teens had set out to annoy the Minister...........an example being that during the tedious Sunday services, they would let the minister's cows out among the growing oats of the glebe (i.e. the church farm lands). It seems that this Rev James Mitchell came off worst in the quarrel for unlike the majority of his predecessors who had died in office, he had had to go.

---

[7] The Story of Glenisla, David Grewer, 1926 p 89

"Thomas Ogilvie was styled a Laird..."

The Duncan's festival season was not quite finished. England and Scotland were still using the Julian calendar - the Gregorian calendar had been instituted by Pope Gregory in 1582, it had the advantage of keeping the months in sync with the seasons, but it was not adopted in Protestant countries as it was seen as a Catholic institution. Yuletide or Christmas was celebrated on the fifth of January until a British act of Parliament finally brought in the Gregorian calendar in 1752. In Craighead where Janet and Andrew were now living, Christmas Eve was celebrated with Sowens Nicht. The young people of the farm toun on January the fourth would have gone from house to house drinking the sowens and eating what food there was.

Sowens, said to be good for the body and the soul, were made

from the rough part of the oat, the husks and the seed, which would be retrieved from the miller when the grain had been milled. It was made by steeping the husks, seeds of oats together with some fine oat meal in water for about a week until the mixture turned sour, then strained and the husks thoroughly squeezed to extract all the meal. A jelly like liquor is left for a further period to ferment and separate, the solid glutinous matter which sinks to the bottom being the sowens, the liquid being the swat . Country folk would prepare the household's sowens weekly. The sowens would often be prepared for eating by boiling with water and salt and eaten like porridge. Sowens could vary depending on the care taken and there was a proverb repeated if a guest felt he had not been entertained properly that went:
"Our sowns are ill sowr'd, ill seil'd. ill salted, ill soden, thin and few of them".

The finished product should apparently be like pea soup. On a special occasion the jelly like liquor obtained after straining and fermentation would be prepared for drinking by heating but not boiling; or they might eat a sowen scone made with swats in the place of milk.

After these two weeks of wedding and Christmas excitement the Duncan's had a few more months of cold short winter days to settle down to married life. Their home was a low, stone walled dwelling, perhaps twenty-four feet long and fourteen foot wide. The roof, resting on V-shaped supports of rough tree timbers, would be thatched with turf, gorse or corn stalks. It could have two front doors of plain rough sawn boards (possibly from stunted Scottish fir tree) with iron hinges and fastened with a sneck, secured at night time by slotting an interior wooden bar across it. One of these doors led in to the house and the other to the cattle byre - this was an improvement on a hundred years before when one door would have served both animals and people.[8]

One of the more astonishing features that did remain on into the nineteenth century was the midden, which often ran along the front of the dwelling with just a six foot or so wide causeway separating it from the door ways and the window of the house. This midden, an excavation of about two feet deep filled with the excrement of animals and humans used to fertilize the crops, was often a semi liquid "unsavory mass" into which it was easy enough to fall.

The "dry closet" or "privy" was a flimsy wooden structure adjacent to the midden where it could be easily emptied in to. The midden itself was emptied only once a year.

---

[8] The homes of the rural population of the Lowlands improved a hundred years before those in the more remote parts of the Highlands. In 1803 a schoolteacher from Rugby in England visited the Western Highlands and described the habitations as "the most destitute and deplorable that the mind can conceive......They are constructed of loose stones, with no upper chambers, no window that opens, or that is large enough to enlighten the rooms; there is no chimney, and no wall or partition in many of them. The smoke escapes by a hole in the thatch, if it escapes at all...." Even in 1836 the New Statistical Account reported of this area that " The houses of the people in general have but one outer door, and as they and their cattle go in by that one entrance - the bipeds to take possession of one end of the house , and the quadrupeds of the other - it cannot be expected that a habitation common to man and beast can be particularly clean. Some of the people , indeed, are now getting into the way of building byres for their cattle, contiguous to their dwelling-houses; and it is acknowledged , even by the most indolent, that a great improvement is thus effected." ref. Pigeon Holes of Memory p 49. Further more these 18th century farm cottages , unlike their English counterparts, did not last in to the 20th century, the country dwellings seen today were constructed in the 19th century.

Photo: Angus Archives, Cultural Services

glassless window with shutters for bad weather. Inside the floor was of earth, the walls were not plastered and there was no ceiling below the rafters, although there may be a few planks for storing food.

The main feature was the fireplace on the end wall. Fuelled with peat these were open fireplaces with a big internal clay chimney. A dark corner of the kitchen, the peat neuk, would hold the peat needed for the day. There were raised binks or benches on either end. Cooking utensils were hung on a crook suspended from the iron frame that swung in and out. The crook hung on a chain with large round links and could be adjusted to any height.

The cook pots were made of cast iron, blackened with use.

There was the large round bottomed three legged kail pot, kale being a type of heartless cabbage vegetable. Meat was a rarity, the bulk of their diet centred round oatmeal. Similar cast iron, locally made pots were for the oatmeal based dishes of sowens, brochan and skirlie.

The sowens was eaten as a kind of flummery (a soft jelly) or could be used to make ale. Brochan was a gruel, either thick or thin, of oatmeal and water, additions such as rich salt butter or honey - with leeks it was known as a poor person's meal - in fact there was a saying "never bless brochan" meaning that brochan is not worth saying grace for because poor food comes as a right. Skirlie was a similar dish of oatmeal mixed with chopped onions and fried suet or fat in a pan.

There was a fry pan and a griddle for oat cakes as well as a gridiron for oaten bannocks and finally a black iron kettle.

The peat fire was never allowed to go out. At night the live ashes were raked into a pile and covered with ashes which could be roused into a blaze with the puff of the bellows in the morning. The peat smoke, with its pungent odour would hang over the houses on a still day in a blue vapour. Inside this peat smoke smell permeated everything, including the cloths of the folk such that they carried this odour with them everywhere.

Bathrooms were unknown, there might have been a single large wooden tub in the farm "toun" of Craighead which could be commandeered for the occasional clean-up such as prior to a wedding. To expose ones pores by sitting in a hot tub was feared by many as a means of catching disease. It was thought the best way to avoid absorbing infections was to put on a clean linen shirt. So the tub was likely used more often for scrubbing the linen rather than the body.

The table would hold the earthen ware plates, the tankards and spoons - no knives and forks - the spoons were precious being obtained from travelling tinkers and made from fashioned horn. The benches, the spinning wheel and reel and the chests containing clothes and finally a box bed for the married couple and perhaps the youngest child were pretty much the total furnishings. The rest of the family slept on the floor beside the fire.

Box beds at the Angus Museum cottages at Glamis.......the furnishings here probably 19th not 18th century and far better than Andrew and Janet would have had.

A minister, the Rev Thomas Somerville, had somewhat negative memories of these box beds where he would be expected to stay when visiting outlying parishioners. They were he said "fitted with sliding doors from which air was almost entirely excluded......it was not reckoned any deviation from respect to assign one box to two guests, even although the two gentlemen or two ladies as the case might be, thus assorted, might be before unacquainted with each other or of different age or rank." [9] The beds however must have given some privacy in these one roomed cottages. Where there were not enough beds folk would wrap themselves in blankets and sleep on the floor by the fire embers.

Two last features sometimes found at these country cottages were the "loupin stoun" and the "dais", both outside; the loupin stoun was the mounting block, especially needed when the wife was to climb aboard the pad behind the husband on a horse. The dais was a large stone built in to the wall and covered in turf, where one could sit on a fine day out of the peaty interior and enjoy the sun and the company of passers by. It is not clear whether this dais would be on the side of the building when the frontage was facing the midden.

---

[9] My Own Life and Times 1741-1814 Thomas Somerville p 338

Drawing: Bill Bailey

Cortachy Castle in Glen Clova home of the Ogilvy family . Members of the Ogilvy family were land lords for much of the land farmed by the ancestors of John and Jane Storrier in Glenisla and Lintrathen. The title Earl of Airlie was created on 2 April 1639 for James Ogilvy 7th Lord Ogilvy along with the titles Lord Ogilvy of Alith and Lintrathen. The title Lord Ogilvy of Airlie had been created on 28 April 1491.

Glen Clova and the gardens of "the bonnie hoose of Airlie" became a place for outings for Victorians from Forfar and is still, in the 21st century, the private dwelling of David Ogilvy, the current Earl of Airlie, and his wife.

Chapter 2

The Kirk

The Duncans would have had some socialising each Sunday, on the Sabbath. They went down to Kirk (the church in Glen Isla) which was well attended unless the conditions were particularly obnoxious. People walked or rode on horseback - the wife side saddle behind the farmer - several miles for the social as well as the religious aspect of the Sunday service. Everyone put on their best clothes and first gathered at the hotel across the road from the Kirk where the adults could enjoy an ale, or if they were well to do enough, a French claret or a whisky and a gossip before going in to church.

The church we can visit today was not built until 1823, when it was proudly said to seat 700. The inference is that the church of Andrew and Janet's time was smaller and not as well built. We do know it was well attended even if some of the pews were occupied by those who were "in the world of nod before the "Firstly" had been well got over by the minister ....due to the effects of their long walk and the wee drap of whisky". [10]

There were probably some canine visitors present too since when shepherds attended they were "as regularly encased in their plaid as accompanied by his dog" [11] .The Storrier family,

---

[10] op.cit The Story of Glenisla p51

[11] Russell, James, Reminiscences of Yarrow (1894)

who derived their name from Storar, meaning sheep herder, would have accounted for the presence of several dogs at Glenisla kirk. If you ever wondered why some old church pews have little doors on the end these dogs may have been the reason. "There were no doors on the seats, and nothing but a narrow deal in each as a footboard, and no separation below between them. The planking on the passages was very deficient, a great deal of the earthen floor was thus exposed; and it can easily be imagined that when the shepherds...came to church each man accompanied by his dog - frequent rows ensued. On the slightest growl from one, all pricked up their ears. If a couple of them fell out and showed fight, it was the signal for a general melee. The rest that were prowling about, or half asleep at their masters' feet, rushed from their lairs, found a way through below the pews, and among the occupants , and raised literally such a dust as fairly enveloped them. Then the strife waxed fierce and furious, the noise became deafening, the voice of the minister was literally drowned, and he was fain to pause whether preaching or in prayer. Two or three shepherds had to leave their places and use their nibbies unmercifully before the rout was quelled, and the service of the sanctuary could be resumed." [12]

These Sabbath services were protracted....they could begin at 10.30, and with over an hour of interval may continue until 7pm. However there seems to have been refreshments of bread and cheese and milk provided for all comers at the manse while there was a sumptuous dinner there for the minister and the elders. We do not know what the character of the minister of Glenisla was like in 1740, but we do know that the minister was a man of some status in the community, and often stayed many years. Take the minister of Yarrow who "whether in the

---

[12] ibid,

balmy days of youth or when in the enjoyment of green old age...his commanding appearance and benevolent expression and dignified bearing at all times won the respect of his people and when on a sacramental occasion he walked out in his court dress and cocked hat and powdered hair, there was something more striking and venerable still in the eyes of his rural flock" [13]

The hour's walk back up to Craighead was often in the dark. The Duncans may have been accompanied by John and Elizabeth McKenzie, Grewers and the Mills along with the Storriers, the last leaving them at Craigniety half a mile down the hill from Craighead. We cannot be sure how many families lived at Craighead and Craigniety though settlements were usually based on plough gates, i.e. the number of oxen or horses required to plough the arable land in one year. In this upland region the Scots plough pulled by four horses-"sorry enough specimens" - or oxen. Craighead then likely had four families and as a farm settlement would have been referred to as a toun or town, although it was far from what we would label as a town today.

Over pag:. The Mutch worn by married women, water colour by Henry W Kerr in Dean Ramsay's Reminiscences p 189

---

[13] ibid

The Kirk was the main source of public help for those in need. There were no social services as we know them today and social problems ere referred to the Kirk Session. This was a council made up of elders chosen by the community and led by their minister. They had limited funds to distribute as there was not a lot of cash around. The church had trouble imposing fines of any size and its poor fund had to make do on small collections which often included odd coinage that had to be gathered and sometimes melted down to be of any value.

Early in 1741 the most talked about affair was the Exposed Child. On the 2nd of March, at night, a child was found "left exposed" to the weather - still obviously very cold - in the vicinity of Auchenleish and Brewlands. These were farm "touns" on the other side of the river Isla, a little downstream but well within the Parish of Glenisla. The child, a boy, was alive and needed nursing and it fell to the Kirk Session to find someone to look after the baby. The only public body within the Parish was the Kirk Session and consequently they dealt with many secular as well as sacred matters. The members of the Kirk Session were the Elders, men elected by the parishioners and usually living scattered throughout the Parish. It was unusual therefore for nobody to have any idea where this child came from as between them the Elders would have a personal acquaintance with all of the 1,800 odd folk who lived there.

Early spring was the time when people were most stretched and 1740 had been a bad harvest. Supplies of food and fodder were low and it was reported how "great a burden this child's expenses would be upon the parish, and how unable the parish was at this time for bearing it". So an intense search for the mother of the child was organised within Glenisla and letters were sent asking the ministers in the neighbouring parishes of

Alyth, Lintrathen and Kirkmichael whether they had any knowledge of the origins of this child.

By the 15th of March, having had no success the session obtained a warrant from Bailie Smith empowering one James Robson, Regality Officer or Alexander Butter, Constable's Officer , in conjunction with the an elder , to search for the mother. A constables' officer would be a part time, unpaid person who had been elected by the Parish to keep order. The Regality Officer was appointed by the Bailie who presided over the Regality Court in the capacity of deputy for the Lord of Regality. This presumably was the David Ogilvy, Earl of Airlie whose Scottish residence was in the Parish of Cortachy to the north of Glenisla. It is interesting that it was felt necessary to apply for this warrant to carry out the search. "The Lord of Regality is Judge in Crimes that deserve Death, and may proceed upon Theft, Murder or any other Crimes upon Citation." 1708 [14]

All the investigation failed to find the mother and the child continued to be nursed by a Margaret Lawson, wife of Thomas White - women even after marriage, were frequently always referred to by their maiden names. Alexander Butter, the "constable's officer" applied for he and his wife to care for the childe if there were given five scots pounds and a firlot of meal for the first quarter and five pounds scots a quarter thereafter. A Scots pound was at this time equivalent to one English penny so it was not quite as much as first appears. However the session did not consider Mrs Butter to be a "fit person to take charge of the child" [15]and they offered these terms to Thomas White and Margaret Lawson who duly accepted.

---

[14] Dictionary of Scots Language

[15] The Story of Glenisla op cit p 102

By now they were in to October of 1741 and had to set about having special collections at church to cover these costs. The first Sabbath set aside for this it was so cold and so few attended that not enough was raised and the exercise had to be repeated. The kirk session records show that the case of the exposed child was not dropped in the following years, different leads arose and rewards were offered and eventually the mother was thought to be Elizabeth Dewar of Glenfernate from Atholl. It was suspected that she had an accomplice who had been prepared to over look the child much as the mother of Moses had stayed hidden in the bull rushes to ensure the child was found and did not die of exposure. However this last was never proven and Elizabeth herself disappeared into the labyrinth of the poor in Edinburgh.

There was a sad conclusion to the story as written in an entry of 9 March 1746 "It being reported that the exposed child died on the 13th of February last there was given for his coffin £1 Scots and refreshment for those who carried the corpse fourteen shillings".[16]

Andrew and Janet's first born, Thomas, arrived in 1742 and their second child Ann the following year in 1743.It does not appear that Andrew and Janet had practised the eighteenth century Highland custom of hand fasting where the couple lived together for a year and a day before deciding on whether to wed, it being most important that the bride was fertile. The Duncan children, Thomas and Ann, were taken to Glenisla for baptism though it appears that not all births were recorded. Some years later in 1759 the church was saying how important it was to register baptisms and parents were urged to give the

[16] Ibid p109

names of offspring to the Minister or session clerk as soon as possible if bad weather or distance was preventing them attending church.

painting in Angus Folk Museum, Glamis

Whether Andrew and Janet continued to go to church at this stage in their lives we do not know. Certainly there was not room for everyone in the parish to attend..........it may have been that those attending the morning three hour service were different from those attending the equally long afternoon one. Either way the church did not accommodate all the inhabitants (1,800 or so) ; it did however seem to have a good deal of influence on everyday life.

There was a strong element of theatre in many Parish churches with the ministers eloquently warning of the pits of hell awaiting those communities who were not among the chosen.

The seventeenth century pulpits had plenty of fire and brimstone warnings and when in the eighteenth century a new generation of more moderate graduates came along it was not always appreciated, as when an older minister was sympathised with for his newly ordained son's efforts: "We all feel wae your mishap, reverend sir, but it canna be concealed your silly loon Frank has fashed a' the congregation, wi' his idle cackle; for he has been babbling this 'our about a gude benevolent God, and that the souls o' the heathens themselves will be gang to heaven, if they follow the licht of their conscience. No word did the daft lad ken, speer, nor say aboot the gude and comfortable doctrine o' election, reprobation, original sin and faith. Hoot man, awa wi sic' a fellow". [17]

Moderation was here to stay - so one minister complained he had had to give his sermon to a congregation of six hundred sleeping heads. Better this than the witch hunt fevers that had occurred in Scotland by over zealous believers. Not until 1736 was the repeal of the 1563 Parliament decree for death to anyone practising witchcraft or consulting a witch. For two hundred years there had been waves of witch hunts which resulted in the deaths of over four thousand and the torture of even more.

Some of this had been fuelled by the fierce rhetoric coming from the pulpit every Sunday with visions of damnation for those who were not predestined to go to heaven. True believers were "justified" by their faith and as such were assured of their place on earth and in heaven as members of an elect community. Witches were seen as the devil's agents and whilst Forfarshire does not seem to have been a place where persecutions flourished nearby Perthshire was. (And indeed

---

[17] Scottish Men of Letters in the 18th Century, Henry Grey Graham p 31

part of Perthshire was in Forfarshire, the county which contained Glenisla.)

If a community claimed that a woman was a witch a confession of guilt was required so that she could be put on trial. Sometimes the woman would confess voluntarily, but if she did not the procedure was to get one from her by torture. These could be horrifically severe: breaking irons, thumbscrews, preventing sleep; or a man with special skills in the "art" or pricking would prick her all over until he found a "witch mark" which was a place on her body that was insensitive to pain. Such a witch mark was taken as proof that the woman was a servant of the devil. It was believed that witches worked in groups of thirteen so the woman would be asked to name the other members of her coven. By this time, crazed with pain, she would call out any names known to her and these women would brought and subjected to the same torture.

The last witch to be strangled was in 1727 (not so very long ago) and this for the "crime" that she had turned her daughter in to a pony............Andrew and Janet were living in what we would call more rational time. The church could impose small fines on people, it could excommunicate them, but it could not imprison. It could also make it very difficult for someone to shift in to another Parish for when this was done a character letter of referral was given from one Minister to the next, and without this the new Parish would not accept the new arrivals. As the story of the exposed child shows these were tight communities where everyone knew everyone else's business. The main penalty, and the one which gave great power to the church, was the social ostracism which could be imposed.

Adultery, which seems to have been more frowned upon than fornication, was punishable by the adulterers having to turn up for church each week for up to six months, sometimes in bare feet and dressed in sack cloth, and sit on the "cutty stool" or stool of repentance.

Another offence which could provoke a trial by the Kirk - for the accused were given the chance to defend themselves - was the breaking of the rest on the Sabbath day. For example David Butter and John Lamond[18] had gone to Dundee to purchase grain and had arranged to get it ground in to meal at Meigle on their return. Having been delayed they ended up travelling on a Sunday with the following consequences: - it was recorded on the Kirk Session records that on August 2nd 1741 that the Minister reported a "flagrant noise" arising from "David Butter and John Lamond, their travelling on Sabbath, the 13th of July last, by the church and other places, on their way homeward with loads upon their horses, to the great offence of many who at that time were on their way to attend the ordinances of religion." They were summoned to appear to a meeting of he session and eventually appeared on August 9th 1741:

".............. David Butter and John Lamond, who acknowledged that they did carry meal on the 13th of July, being Sabbath day, that they were sorry it happened so, and resolved to be cautious in time coming of giving public offence. But alleged for themselves that there was an absolute necessity for it, they having left their houses on Thursday without meal, and being so long delayed on the road by rain as only to get homeward to Meigle on Saturday, where they resolved to grind their corn, that they might have it for use that night; which they say they could have done had they got as

---

[18] possibly a brother of Elizabeth Lamond who married John McKenzie at Craighead.

ready service as was promised them. But they were kept so long there that it was Sabbath morning before they got their corn ground.

They were told that if they had brought as much as might support their families till Monday, and left the rest in some safe place till then, this would have prevented the offence that was taken.

-To which they answered that they knew not a safe hand in these straitening times with whom they could entrust their meal.

The session, maturely deliberating on this affair, and hoping that what they had done did not proceed from contempt of the Lord's Day or any design of giving scandal, they were cautioned against giving any unnecessary offence in time coming, and it was agreed that this whole transaction be read from the pulpit next Lord's Day as a caution to others".

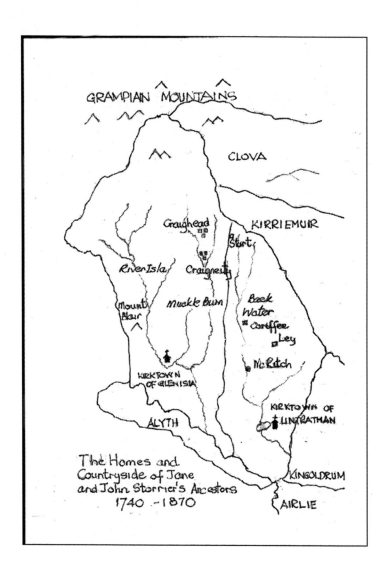

The Homes and
Countryside of Jane
and John Storrier's Ancestors
1740 - 1870

Chapter 3

Farming in the Glens

Tucked away at the head of the glen, Craighead and Craigniety were not at the forefront of agricultural Improvement, as the modernization of farming was termed.. When Andrew and Janet were bringing their children in to the world the farming methods remained essentially communal, as they had been for hundreds of years. The Duncan, McKenzie, Grewer and Mills

---

[19] 1640 map of Glenisla habitations , visible is the symbol for the Kirk and the settlements of Craigniety and Sturt where folk in this story were to live. Perhaps once there was an important dwelling at Craigniety , in any event the window lintels for the ruins at Craigneity today are surprisingly large chiselled stone ones. In the 16th century Coupar Abbey was the landlord of Glenisla and the Abbot and brethren of Coupar Abbey reserved accommodation for themselves at Dalvanie and Craigniety when they visited the glen on business , or to hunt the "tod and wolf".[#]

families would have been working in a system where "everyone claims an equal share in the direction", a system which was most frowned upon by the advocates of Improvement. Where traditional farming methods were used, according to Sir John Sinclair and a great number of writers in the seventeenth and early eighteenth centuries, it meant that "all attempts of improvement were in vain".[20]

Between them the families of Craighead and those at Craigniety which included the Storrier family, would have had enough ponies or oxen to do the ploughing required in one year. "Craig" meant highlands and Craighead and Craigniety were situated on the spur of land between two streams which ran down to join the river Isla near the Kirkton of Glenisla. This area was between fifty and one hundred acres depending exactly where the boundaries came and probably required eight oxen or ponies. Their cattle, sheep, possibly goats and ponies would have been smaller, poorer specimens than those seen on these hills today.

There were possibly a dozen families living here and sharing this plough team; for this number of people to gain a living from such a small area required what could be described as sophisticated co-operative organisation. Eighteenth century writers described it as "barbaric"; now, looking back with a space of two hundred years and knowing the problems which arise from urbanisation it could be seen as idyllic. Certainly it was a method which enabled a large number of people to subsist quite happily and to live in the country. While landlords

---

[20] Sir John Sinclair was the editor of the Statistical Accounts of 1790/91 and 1834 which heavily influenced most historical thinking thereafter see T.M. Devine The Scottish Nation pg124 et seq

needed a large number of tenants, either to fight for them or, as was more the case by 1700, to periodically work for them on their farms, the tenants had a type of insurance in knowing that their landlord[21] would support them in times of great hardship rather than lose his tenants.

Essential to the system were the "commonties", land where animals could be grazed, peat for fuel could be gathered at no cost other than that of their labour, and likewise the building materials of stone, turf, bracken and heather. The families would have to agree how many stock could be grazed on the unfenced communal land, the number of animals limited by the extent and quality of the available pasture. Nowadays the hills below these settlements are green with new varieties of grass well fertilized by the lorry load. In Andrew Duncan's day they did know the value of limestone as a fertilizer and that there were large areas of limestone in the area. But it was too costly in terms of fuel to utilise. There were some stone kilns where limestone was put alternating with peat which, when fired, would produce good fertilizer but this method used up too much peat. Richer farmers in Glenisla could fertilize with marle, a calcium carbonate (limestone) rich mudstone which was found in a crumbly form ready to use, but this was at a Loch nine miles away. It had to be brought by the basketful on ponies and was still only used for the infields of those who could afford it.

---

[21] In the middle ages the Abbott of Coupar Abbey was the land lord in Glen Isla. Later the Earl of Airlie (head of the Ogilvy family) became the predominant land owner. Some of the younger members of the Ogilvy family were given land in Glen Isla, By the 19[thcentury] Glen Isla had several smaller land owners whereas almost all the land in Glen Clova had the Earl of Airlie (the Ogilvys) as landlord. The families in this story did not own the land they farmed.

Can the lady handle a creel? - was a question asked of a potential wife, meaning would she have the strength to load up the large wicker baskets slung on either side of a pony and get the manure from the midden out on to the fields - and likewise cut the peat and bring that in. The cutting of peat, the essential fuel, was another job that needed careful communal agreement so that it was done in such a way that over the years it would regenerate so that the same areas yielded good peat over the generations.

Most stock would have to be sold before winter when feed was restricted to the sparse hay brought in from the rough boggy meadows down by the streams below Craighead and Craigniety. Sometimes the cattle, who had been kept in the byres over winter (and possibly bled to provide extra food for the family) would be so weak that they would have to be carried out to their spring pastures. This day was called "the liftin'".

The land around their dwellings was most likely laid out in a mosaic of patches. There were the fertilized areas for growing the cabbage vegetable, kale. The inclusion of a green vegetable which could be successfully grown in this area had been recognised as an essential since medieval times. In New Zealand Captain Cook was thought to be the revolutionary nutritionist who discovered the importance fresh fruit or vegetables played in the diet. In the early sixteenth century the land lord of Craighead and Craigniety, the Abbott of Coupar, compelled all the tenants as part of their rental agreement to grow kale as a defense against "scorbutic affections" - (this the Latin word for scurvy, a deficiency of vitamin C leading to bleeding gums, depression and ultimately immobilisation of the liver spotted patient).

Each household would have its own patch of vegetable garden which was fertilized from the midden each year at a time when all were agreed upon to work together. Beyond this was another area which would have been fertilized in a like manner where the bere was grown. From this hardy but low yielding strain of barley ale would be brewed. The land would be ploughed up in wide strips , called run rig. The weeds and stones formed a ridge, the rig, where the crop was sown by hand; between each rig the run where the water could drain. These ridge and furrows, were reinforced by the method of ploughing. Big stones could mark the boundaries of different users. So within one area of plough different families would be assigned their particular ridges; each family's assigned land was thus scattered over the various areas under plough thus ensuring no single family had the best or the worst areas. They also took turns, sometimes drawing lots, for these strips. One of the criticisms of this method of farming being that there was no incentive to improve your land - for example keeping it weeded, since it was unlikely to be yours long term. "Guld" or corn marigold, was considered the worst weed - it was acid tolerant and repressed grain crops plus it prevented rapid drying of cut grain as it had a succulent stem.

Another criticism was that each farmer's arable land was in strips often scattered over a wide area. Nor was there any systematic rotation of crops to include a fallow period to regularly rest the land. Land then tended to be worked until it was totally unproductive then let to go wild. These lands were termed the in-field and did not lie in a neat pattern. They could appear as quite haphazard patches in the open fields

Vestiges of the run rig system. This photo in the neighboring Glen Prosen shows nineteenth century stone enclosure walls and twentieth century wire reinforcements.

surrounding the houses. [22]Usually the ridge and furrows would be running vertically for drainage. This is a wet country - as one eighteenth century traveller noted when he met a local clergyman who said "generally speaking the climate may be termed damp" , a remark from which the traveller concluded "that the man was a humorist, conscious or unconscious, of the first water...."[23]

Further out and not always so deeply ploughed was the outfield, an area where the staple food crop of oats was sown.

---

[22] The Scottish and English rural habitations were different: the latter had nucleated villages surrounded by fields where a 3 year rotation of winter rye, summer barley and fallow land was followed; Scottish hamlets were scattered and had this infield and outfield system with no fallow. See Scottish Farming Past and Present, J A Symon p17.

[23] Letters from a Gentleman in the North of Scotland, Edward Burt pg 17

The plough used was an old wooden scotch plough with iron points and drawn by up to four small ponies or oxen. One man walked backwards controlling the ponies or oxen and another walked behind working the plough. These dray animals would be owned and used communally. To reach agreement on such matters as when these tasks should he done it was frequently decided to use traditional dates, a method that, with the vagaries of climate, could be disadvantageous.

The type of oat grown, the poor soils and the harsh climate meant that the yields were only for the consumption of these farmers, there was none left for selling. Indeed it has been said that for each grain of oat sown there were but three produced: one for the farmer, one for the rent and the third to be kept for the following year's seed. The lightness of the crop meant a poor harvest would be followed by a second hard year as frequently all the seed crop had been devoured in the winter.

Ox plough, photographed here in Angus Folk Museum, Glamis.

In early summer stock could be confined at night within a small temporary enclosures made from sods and loose stones and this would provide manure for fertilization. There were no protective dykes or hedges for shelter and no fences to keep animals out of the crops grown in either the in or out fields. Hence the value of young children who could herd the sheep or cattle.

In summer when the crops were ripening some wives and children took the herded stock higher up on to common land and stayed in rough earth and rock huts. These shielings would have thatched roofs and the ubiquitous peat fire described the traveler thus: "on a raised hearth in the center of the floor burned a merry kindly looking peat fire with its soft fringe of white and orange ashes".[24]

Being awarded the task of going with the stock to the higher pastures seems like a pleasant way to spend the summer and for children it was an accepted reason for not attending school. Up in the high hills cranberries and the averin berry could be picked when found, the averin berry was particularly delicious but did not keep. Down by their home the rowan tree could be stripped of its berries and made in to jam if there was sugar enough.

The only fly in the ointment may have been the infamous midge which appears to have been as much in evidence then as now - our eighteenth century traveller: "I do not hesitate to say, that within a radius of say ten yards about us, the number of the midges was at least equal to the present population of the Chinese Empire, whatever that may be. How many we slew

---

[24] ibid pg 71

with our hands; how many we swallowed, how many committed suicide before our eyes on our oil canvasses, it is impossible to say; but one strange fact impressed us greatly. As the hours went by we could detect no diminution whatever, not even of a single midge, in the myriad hosts of our assailants."[25] Presumably the locals had ways of evading the bites of the midges. At least in early 1745 if this was all that was attacking them their worries were few. The poor harvest of the year when Andrew and Janet were married was behind them. Their lives appeared to be following a long established pattern and along with the Grewers, McKenzies and Storriers they could look forward to living in the Glen.

---

[25] ibid pg 84

Chapter 4

Jacobites in Glenisla and Lintrathen

'Twas on a Monday morning
Right early in the year
That Charlie cam to our town
The young chevalier
An' Charlie is my darling
My darling, my darling
Charlie is my darling
The young Chevalier.

Then ik a bonnie lassie say
As to the door she ran
Our king shall hae is ain again
An Charlie's the man;
For Charlie he's my darling…..

Our Highland hearts are true an' leal
An glow without a stain;
Our Highland swords are metal keen
An Charlie he's our ain
An Charlie he's my darling….

This song was published in the nineteenth century in a book entitled Jacobite Relics. It reflects the romantic nostalgia that had by then coloured the records of these times. In 1745 not all Highlanders welcomed the Chevalier's arrival.

By July 1745, when Bonnie Prince Charlie raised his standard at Glenfinnan up on the Western Isles, Andrew and Janet's children would have been three and two years old. There is no record of Andrew joining the Jacobites[26], and it is unlikely any joined the Government troops from Glenisla; but it is not inconceivable that he joined the Jacobites in the excitement of that summer.

The Kirk session records are silent on the matter, their interest remaining on the keeping of the Sabbath as they report that "on the 11th current [i.e. August1745] Margaret Lawson, Thomas McInnes and John McKenzie [possibly of Craighead] had profaned the Lord's Day by unnecessarily going to the hill and gathering of berries, the officer was appointed to summon them to appear before the session against the 1st Sept. next". McKenzie duly appeared, and, on confessing fault and promising never to do the like in time coming, was rebuked and dismissed. The other two appearing later were similarly dealt with."[27]

While the written records remain concentrated on matters such as the breaking of the Sabbath there must have been discussions at the Glenisla Inn as the Jacobite cause gathered momentum. The Innkeeper himself, James Rioch, was a volunteer. The Glenisla folk would have been aware of Charles' progress south as he successfully went from Perth down to Edinburgh in September where he kept court at Holyroodhouse.

There were some landlords who constrained their tenants to

---

[26] an extensive research by David Dobson "The Jacobites of Angus" 1689-1746 pts 1 and 2 do not bring up his name.

[27] The Story of Glenisla op cit p 157

join up and even at this stage there were some who had had enough and deserted. For example Lord George Murray wrote home urging his nephew to destroy the houses and crops of deserters as an example to others.[28] It does not seem that any landlords were thus inclined in Glenisla.

The ousting of the direct Stuart[29] line from the thrones of England Scotland and Wales in 1688 was lamented by the Scots. Yet not all were anxious to see this line reinstated. The current Hanoverian monarch George II was there as the nearest blood relative who was of the protestant faith. A catholic monarch might try to justify absolute power over his subjects, raise taxes directly, by pass elected parliaments, and impose a Popish church in place of the Presbyterian Church of Scotland.

The Stuart allegiance to the "superstitions of the Popish church" was going to cause ambivalence in a Parish where the Kirk was as strong as it was in Glenisla. The Church of Scotland had provided a strong network of Ministers trained in Calvinistic thought which differed both in organisation and theology from either the Roman Catholics or the English Episcopalians[30]. Indeed should a Stuart monarch take over the current minister could have lost his comfortable livelihood, and the Elders of the church their power. The Glenisla parish was unlikely to have had pro Jacobite sermons in Kirk on Sundays.

---

[28] see J.D. Mackie A History of Scotland p 277

[29] an explanation for the change from Stewart to Stuart is that the French did not have a "W" in their alphabet and after the beheading of Charles 1 the Stewart/Stuart "Pretenders" were largely based in France.

[30] Episcopalian church organisation was through the appointment from above of Bishops which, if the King could control these nominations gave power to the crown. The Church of Scotland gave more power to the parishioners who elected their leaders.

What then would cause men to take up arms? Discontent due to food shortages had not caused riots as it had in coastal burghs and in any event the bad harvests of 1740-41 were over. There was the motivation of increased taxation which could have led some to want a change in government, a sentiment expressed by Robert Freebairn as follows:

"Before the Union [i.e. 1707 Union of English and Scottish Parliaments] we had no Taxes but were laid on by our own Parliaments, and those very easie, and spent within our own Country. Now we have not only the Cess or Land Tax, and Customs conform to the English Book of Rates, near the Triple what we formerly pay'd, and Excise, both most rigorously exacted by a Parcel of Strangers sent down to us from England, but also the Malt-Tax, the Salt-Tax, the Leather-Tax, the Window-Tax, the Taxes upon Candles, Soap, Starch.....the Tax upon stamped Paper and Parchments, most,,,of which are bound upon us for 64, and some of them for 99 years to come.....".[31]

Nevertheless it is unlikely that the increases in the price of salt and beer which Janet and Andrew would have had to pay would have been enough to make them and others with homes in Glenisla want to go to war. Nor did the Ogilvy landlords resort to force as Lord Lewis Gordon was purported to have done "raising men, and levying money by force and threats of military execution, in the shires of Bamff and Aberdeen."[32]

Whatever the reason it appears that most of the men kept their heads down when the call came to fight for Bonnie Prince Charlie, son of the Old Pretender, James Stuart. Out of a population of nearly two thousand just eleven or twelve

---

[31] The Miserable State of Scotland, Robert Freebairn Perth 1720
[32] Proceedings of the Jacobites in the North www.electricscotland

Glenisla men are recorded as having gathered to join the Ogilvy Regiment. The only labourer [33] was George Grewer, a soldier ;then there were Andrew Samson and John Edward "in Glenisla" but of unknown occupation . There were two Thomas Ogilvys of East Mill one of whom was a Captain and the other an Ensign for the Ogilvy Regiment. An "artful rogue" John Coutts from Woodend joined for the plunder, having little interest in the Stuart or Hanoverian monarchy.

Other volunteers were the Glenisla innkeeper, James Rioch and two farmers, John Robertson of Crandart and William Shaw from Forter along with his brother Alexander Shaw. Finally there was William Farquharson of Broughdearg in Glenshee who also farmed at West Mill and Doonie in Glenisla. [34] The Farquharson family, like the Ogilvys, were historically loyal supporters of the Jacobites .

These men were part of one of two battalions raised in Angus. The first set out from Edinburgh [35] marching in to England in

---

[33] The Jacobites of Angus 1689-1746 Part One and Two op cit contains a comprehensive list of those who were recorded as having fought or aided the Jacobites

[34] Ibid

[35] The fighting was not a war between the Englishmen and the Scots. The Government army had a large Hanoverian contingent. And there were many Scotsmen who supported the Government forces. John Home who was in Edinburgh when the Jacobites arrived describes the scene:: "the rebel [Jacobites] were at hand, and a wonderful band of 400 or 500 volunteers was raised to defend the city - an awkward squad of students, law clerks, domestically minded citizens, possessed of fluctuating courage, to whom the firing of a musket with closed eyes with aim in to space was an agitating effort.....supported by two regiments of dragoons, they mustered with trembling hearts, their wives and mothers protesting with tears that their husbands and sons, were too precious to be slaughtered by Highland villains. When the order came to march to the West Bow was given officers

early November of 1745, the second joining up before the battle of Falkirk in January of 1746. Altogether they provided seven hundred men. There were five and a half thousand men in the Jacobite army when they crossed the border into England in November.

By contrast the neighbouring parish of Lintrathen supplied at least thirty eight men the majority of whom were workmen, labourers, ploughmen and servants; there were four farmers, a miller and various members of the Ogilvy family all led by David Ogilvy, son of the Earl of Airlie.

The Earl of Airlie, John Ogilvy, was the principle land owner in this area and the Ogilvy family had been staunch Jacobites and followers of the Roman Catholic faith. The parish of Lintrathen had a smaller population than Glenisla - one thousand odd - but probably there were more tenants of the Ogilvy family who could be pressed in to service.[36] There were fewer independent heritors (land owners) in Lintrathen than in Glenisla. Also in 1790 the church was described as "an old, dark, disproportioned fabrick....the manse...a wretched hovel......situated at the southern extremity of the Parish which had no town, no village, no innkeeper, no baker, no

---

complained that the men would not follow, and the men murmured that the officers would not lead." John Home was himself a minister of the church (and an angler, a playwright and needless to say, popular figure) . He describes how he and his comrades went to join Sir John Cope...calling at every alehouse to drink in a choppin of two penny or a mutchkin of brandy confusion to the Pretender; how they slept comfortably the night before a battle in a manse only to wake up and find the fight was over; that the volunteers had fled before the violent charge of highland cavalry, consisting of three or four gentlemen with their servants in full pursuit." Scottish Men of Letters pg 60-1

[36] There were just 5 land owners, heritors, in 1790 in Lintrathen, and all of them absentee landlords. Stat.acc.1791p564

surgeon, no butcher, no apothecary ....".[37] It would seem the Ogilvys had not done much to support the Church of Scotland within Lintrathen.

Among the Lintrathen soldiers were members of the Farquharson family including James. James was twenty three and already married to Elspeth Low; they had a son Robert born between 1742 and 1745[38]. James and Elspeth were to be linked to the Glenisla Duncan's in the following century, forming the Lintrathen strand of the Forfarshire family that left Scotland to live in New Zealand.

James was the son of Maren Lindsay and James Farquharson who was a farmer at Westertoun in Lintrathen. The home he grew up in would have been similar to that of Andrew and Janet Duncan's and this is the place he is recorded as coming from when he entered the army as number 25OR (Ogilvy Regiment). The Jacobite records say "James Farquharson, the son of James Farquharson (farmer) was pressed to serve in Lord Ogilvy's Regiment". Pressed, rather than volunteering implies he did not necessarily want to go; was he obliged to on the terms his family held the farm tenancy? This would not have been surprising had Ogilvy owned Westertoun, but in fact this land had been sold in Mr John Kinlock around 1700 .

Nevertheless when James joined up the troops were in good spirit. Prince Charlie, was just twenty four years old and full of vitality and optimism. He was sure his benefactor King Louis XV of France would , sooner or later, front up with the needed six thousand French troops, arms for ten thousand more and a war chest of thirty thousand louis d'or . Young Charles had not

---

[37] Statistical Account no.xxxv pg 563

[38] A Highland Heritage, Jean Hay, p 62

been deterred by the fact that he had had to land at Loch Shiel, Glenfinnan in July of 1745 with a few companions, limited arms and just four thousand gold coins.

At first his confidence appeared justified. Gathering support, he travelled rapidly south using General Wade's military roads[39]. The government garrisons had been emptied of troops to fight in Europe where they had had success against the French. It was the hope that a Scottish uprising would take battle hardened soldiers out of Europe back to Britain and allow the French to get rid of the Hanoverian power that had stimulated the French king's support of the Jacobite cause. By September the Jacobites had taken Edinburgh and gone on to a victory at Prestopan. There is a curious tale of Prestopan arising from an aversion the Highlanders were said to have of pigs: Lord Elco who fought with the Prince recorded - "All that day [i.e. the eve of Prestopan] people ran great risk of being shot by the highlandsmen, for as they think it Ominous to let hogs or hares pass their lines, they kill'd several of them to the great risk of Everybody that was near."[40] In November they were in England and advancing on Carlisle.

Robertson of Crandart, one of the farmers from Glenisla, was reputed to be the handsomest man in the Highland army. He

---

[39] "After the first Jacobite uprisings (1708-1719) General Wade had been sent to subdue the Highlands and in order to do this he had embarked on an ambitious scheme to open up the country by making roads. One such road from Inverness to Fort William General Wade drove along in a coach and six horses to the great wonder of the inhabitants who, before this road was made, could not pass on horseback without danger and difficulty. So the man who had been sent to civilize the Highlanders had actually provided them, and Bonnie Prince Charlie, with roads at no cost or trouble to themselves." Pigeon Holes of Memory p29

[40] Pigeon Holes of Memory Dr John McKenzie p 39 and 48

apparently got on well with the Prince and was said to be at the Prince's right hand when walking victoriously in to Carlisle. He later married Margaret Farquharson, the daughter of his fellow campaigner, William Farquharson. The entrée in to Carlisle was however the beginning of the end for as the army marched south it became increasingly obvious that they were not going to be joined by enthusiastic supporters to the anti Hanovarian cause. The only regiment to join them was a mainly Catholic one from Manchester. They did reach as far south as Derby by early December. However the weather was deteriorating, the funds running out, the French had only sent a token support force of three ships with relatively few munitions. Then messengers foretold the immanent arrival of efficient troops which had been brought back from Europe to meet the Jacobite challenge. There seemed no alternative but to backtrack.

They had in fact to use all their tactical and fighting skills to get back to Scotland. At Falkirk in January amidst torrential rain they turned and fought the government forces. The ensuing fight was a victory for the Jacobites although not all the troops were aware of this for some time. The battle which was fought on the south muir of the town was described by one chevalier Johnson - " the most singular and extraordinary combat ......the Highlanders, stretched on the ground, thrust their dirks into the bellies of the horses. Some seized the riders by their clothes, dragged them down and stabbed them with their dirks,; several again used their pistols, but few of them had sufficient space to handle their swords. The resistance of the Highlanders was so incredibly obstinate that the English, after having been for some time engaged pell-mell with them in their ranks were at length repulsed and forced to retire." It was all over in less than an hour and later that night Johnston returned with a sergeant and twenty men to guard the captured cannons on the battlefield: " The sergeant carried a lantern; but the light was soon extinguished and by that accident we immediately lost our way, and wandered a long time at the foot of the hill, among heaps of dead bodies [there were over three hundred dead red coats and about forty dead Jacobites] which their whiteness rendered visible....To add to the disagreeableness of our

Falkirklocalhistory.co.uk

situation from the horror of the scene, the wind and the rain were full in our faces. I even remarked a trembling and strong agitation in my horse, which constantly shook when it was forced to puts its feet on the heaps of dead bodies and to climb over them...on my return to Falkirk I felt myself relieved from an oppressive burden; but the horrid spectacle I had witnessed was for a long time fresh in my mind ." [41]

---

[41] Chevalier de Johnston Memoirs of the Rebellion 1745-46 from Angus or Forfarshire Part xiv by A.J. Warden FSA.

Falkirk may have been a success on the day but it did not stem the retreat to the highlands even on the aftermath of the battle. One anecdote tells much of the naivety, the lack of training and suitable weaponry of these Jacobite soldiers:

"The Highlanders, pleased with the fire-arms they had picked up upon the field of battle, were frequently handling and discharging them. Afraid of accidents, the officers had issued orders prohibiting this abuse, but to no purpose. One .....had secured a musket which had been twice loaded. Not aware of this circumstance, he fired off the piece, after extracting one of the balls, in the direction of some officers who were standing together on the street of Falkirk. The other ball unfortunately entered the body of 'Neas Macdonell, second son of Glengary........he survived only a short time, and satisfied of the innocence of the man that shot him, begged with his last breath that he might not suffer.

"To soothe the Glengary men under their loss, the Prince evinced by external acts that he participated in their feelings, and, to show his respect for the memory of this brave and estimable youth, attended his funeral as chief mourner; but nothing the prince was able to do could prevent some of the men, who felt more acutely than others the loss of the representative of their chief, from returning to their homes."[42]

Many soldiers, lacking arms, with their artillery ditched and having to spread out wide to find their own food, broke ranks and returned home. After Falkirk a strong leader in the Duke of Cumberland took over the government army comprising of disciplined Hanovarian soldiers as well as pro government Scots. Cumberland's troops, unlike Charles', were supplied from sea and he was able to steadily follow the harried Prince Charles and mainly Highlander Jacobite troops up the East

---

[42] www.electricscotland.com/history/falkirk/battle14.html

Coast. A good few Lintrathen and Glenisla men may well have slipped off home on the way .

Whether James Farquharson left during the muddle and rain of the Falkirk engagement (which in fact only lasted a brief half hour or so) or whether he was one of the many who "melted" away between Falkirk and Culloden, we do not know. He and five or six other Farquharsons from Lintrathen left the army, and James at least was recorded as having deserted. Perhaps James was injured, in any event he died at the relatively young age of thirty six and although Elspeth his wife lived on until she was sixty five they never had any children after his return from Falkirk, so his line depended on the survival and marriage of his only son Robert. [43]

Meantime the Prince, deciding against his advisers who suggested dispersing into the hills chose to put his tired and hungry four and a half thousand against Cumberland's well prepared nine thousand soldiers. This lead to the devastating defeat of the Jacobites at Culloden on the sixteenth of April 1746 when two thousand Jacobites compared to three hundred government soldiers were killed.

Those who survived were hunted down, as were all those suspected of helping the Jacobite cause. Charles' charisma had enticed a varied group of supporter, some adventurers, even some disaffected British soldiers, Episcopalian (those who favoured an English style church with Bishops), Roman Catholics, and those loyal to the Stuart blood line as being the true inheritors of the Crown of Scotland and England. The "honourable" aspect of the Jacobite cause and its general support had after the 1715 uprising helped the rebels escape

---

[43] A Highland Heritage, op cit p62

and return to normal life with relative impunity. Not so this time. History was to label the Duke of Cumberland as the butcher of the Scots as he sent his dragoons to search out all who had supported Prince Charles.

Photo:Jacobiterising.devhub.com. Searching for Jacobites after Culloden

In Glenisla they captured George Grewer who was deported from Liverpool along with others from whence he probably ended up a free man in Martinique or Virginia. Andrew Samson and John Edward were also captured there and imprisoned in Dundee. Two fugitives, Oliphant of Gask and his son, managed to hide in Glenisla for six months after which they escaped on a ship to Sweden where they lived in exile for sixteen years.

The ministers of all the Parishes were instructed to furnish the dragoons with a complete list of Jacobites. The Rev. William Arthur we learn "either from compassion or fear, confined his list to seven names". In Forfarshire those Ministers who gave full lists found their manses broken in to and robbed. The names William Arthur gave were men of substance and more able to make good an escape to Sweden or France by paying for a vessel from a port such as Dundee, Montrose or Arbroath.

Care would have to be taken as to who to trust when escaping. There were plenty of supporters for the government, and even within clans or families there were often members who fought on opposite sides. This is illustrated by the following story of the Chevalier de Johnston's escape; as he was fleeing he tried crossing the River Tay south of Glenisla -

"Mr Graham had two nephews in the rebel army......and on hearing of the sad condition of the fugitive, had him brought to an inclosure on his property where there was very high broom. There he visited the Chevalier, apologised for not daring to take him to his Castle of Duntrune on account of his servants, of whose fidelity he was not assured. He promised to get him a boat and food was brought. He...devoured seven or eight eggs in a moment, with a great quantity of bread, butter and cheese, and a bottle of white wine. He had been for seventeen days previously upon oatmeal and water.......after telling him how to proceed, Mr Graham left him............

" He was to follow a gardener to a windmill then an old woman would conduct him to Broughty where there was a ferry crossing across the Tay. .....On reaching the top of the hill above she made him stop until she saw if all was ready, when she would return. After having waited half an hour he left the road, went forward to the brink of the hill , and lay down in a furrow, where he could see the way she would come. A few minutes after he had lain down eight or ten horsemen passed the place he had quitted. She told him the horsemen were dragoons who had searched the village strictly, and had so frightened the boatmen who Mr Graham had employed that they absolutely refused to carry him over. She was so terrified that she was, with difficulty induced to show him the way to the village, and the village inn.

"On entering the public-house the landlady, a Mrs Burn, whispered into his ear that he had nothing to fear in her house, as her own son had been in Lord Ogilvy's clan in the rebel army. She pointed out the boatmen, and he tried much to get them to ferry him over, to no purpose, as they were trembling with alarm at the threats of the soldiers. Two daughters of the landlady, pretty young girls, he flattered, and got to plead with the men, which they did heartily, but with equally little success, after which the girls called them cowards. The elder asked the younger if she would take an oar, and she would take another, and they would row him over, to the shame of the poltroons. At last he took the oars to the boat, pushed it into deep water, took an oar himself, and they girls took the other by turns. They left Broughty at ten o'clock and reached the Fife side before midnight, when the girls landed him, and showed him the road to St Andrews. He offered them money, which they refused, but he contrived to slip ten or twelve shillings into the pocket of the elder and they parted."[44] - One cannot help wondering how long it took the girls to row back............

[44] Angus or Forfarshire part xlv,op cit pg64-65

Broughty Ferry www.oldroadsofscotland.com

Thomas Ogilvy, the Laird of East Miln in Glenisla was not as canny. He had been made a captain in Lord Ogilvy's Regiment "for his zeal in Prince Charles' cause"[45]. After Culloden when he was making his way home he was made a prisoner by troops stationed at Cortachy (Lord Ogilvy's place of residence). From there he was taken to Edinburgh Castle and confined and "despairing of ever being set at liberty, determined to achieve it himself, On the 21st May 1751 he attempted to escape over the walls by means of a net tied to an iron ring, but fell over the rocks and died of a fractured skull."

The leader of the Regiment himself, David Ogilvie did escape from the battlefield and was one of those who sailed from Dundee. He went first to Norway and then on to France. In France he was joined by his wife who had been captured and imprisoned in Edinburgh but had escaped successfully from the castle disguised as her servant. In France David Ogilvy joined the French Army , became a Lieutenant General, and was given a pension from the French Government when he was pardoned by the English government! He returned in in 1778

---

[45] The Story of Glenisla op cit p86

where he died at Cortachy in 1805. The title of Earl of Airlie was not restored until 1826 when it went to another David Ogilvy this time of Clova.

Johnnie Coutts was another who had not been caught. Having found his way back to Glenisla "and for a time lurked among the wilder recesses at the top of the glen…..Finding no safety at home, ..attached himself to a band of caterans and had an oath imposed upon him that he would communicate their intentions to no person. His son became the master mind of the freebooters………" But as Johnnie "did not approve of plundering his native district generally managed to give due warning. Approaching a farm he would attract the attention of someone, and on their approach would turn his back and exclaim loud enough to be heard, "I daurna say't to ony body, but I'm telling' this stane dyke that ther'll likely be an attempt made to lift cattle here the morn's nicht" .

Andrew Duncan may have been the grateful recipient of such a warning as he was vulnerable to such attacks. Craighead was on the side of a valley down which ran a traditional cateran route where stolen cattle were driven. There was still a degree of lawlessness in this area with cattle thieves sometimes posing as dealers. They would visit the farms, look at the cattle, refuse to pay the asking amount, then sneak back at a later date to add to their herds which would be driven to markets far away. This was always in late summer, if they came earlier the cattle would be too weak from the sparse winter fodder to be driven far and fast enough.

A recent booklet written for walkers of the resurrected Cateran trail says the one of the last recorded raids was in 1602. There were tales passed on in the Ogilvy, McKenzie and Grewer families which told of cattle thieves operating after the 1745 rebellion, perhaps as late as 1771. There was said to be a Donald Mor, surnamed Cameron, who, after he was married, became a well known freebooter. On one occasion - probably during a moonlit September night - he drove cattle which he had stolen through the head of Glenisla up an old peat road to the Burn of Corhee where he called a halt. The following day was a fine one for the harvest. The people in the fields of Glen Beg, including one Duncan McKenzie, were cutting their oats and they witnessed a group of some twenty four men in pursuit. Soon after they heard the sound of shots. The pursuers, including John and Andrew Ogilvy, had caught up with the plunderers; and John coming upon Donald Mor sitting with his back to him, had shot him. His bullet went[46] through Donald's skull coming out at the mouth which was full of bread and cheese. Despite this Donald turned on his knees drawing a heavy holster pistol. John called to his brother Andrew to shoot but his gun was empty so he seized the muzzle and brought the doghead down on Donald's head with such force that it split the skull.

It was said that John Murray innkeeper at the Spittal of Glenshee took the bodies down and that there is a tombstone there dated 1771. Donald Mor's jacket had been studded with silver buttons, a regular habit of caterans who did this so that there would always be sufficient money for them to have a christian burial. John Ogilvy ever after went in fear of reprisal, always carrying a gun and when in his own house he would sit facing the door with a loaded gun in his reach.

One last remnant of these 1745 fighters were some tinkers. John McKenzie, born in 1807, remembered families with carts travelling the Highlands, with items for sale. Living as gypsies

---

[46] The Story of Glenisla op cit pg 79-81

but said in this case to have originated as displaced men from the '45 who married and spent their lives travelling. Photo: *celticanamcara.blogspot.co.uk/2010/01scottish-tinkers-and-travellers.html*

Chapter 5
After "the '45" and the Silent Clearances

Andrew Duncan, Charles Grewer, John McKenzie and Andrew Storar (Storrier) of Craighead and Craigneity in Glenisla, and James Farquharson of Lintrathen, would all be linked a hundred years later by John and Jane Storrier who immigrated to New Zealand. Meantime these great grandparents of John and Janespent their lives in the Forfarshire Glens[47].

In December of 1757 the Craighead families celebrated the marriage of Charles Grewer and Isobel Clark. Charles was just 14 years old but this was not considered a bad thing. He must have had the means to support his wife as first child Margaret arrived on 27 October, a year later. After Margaret they had four more girls, roughly every second year, thus adding to the growing population of Scotland.

The mid eighteenth century was when Glenisla's population was at its highest (in 1755 it was 1,852) implying that there was enough food, shelter and work available. Charles Grewer is likely to have been sub-tenant farmer, having obtained the rent of a small dwelling and piece of land from a tenant, rather than himself being a tenant dealing directly with the proprietor. It was from these small "pendicles" of land that from the 1770's on folk would leave in search of a more prosperous life in nearby towns.

---

[47] A map drawn up in 1732 by Herman Moll is labelled The Shire of Angus or Forfar; today the area is call Angus.

By this time Andrew and Janet Duncan had had six children. John McKenzie and his wife Elizabeth Lamond also had six children including young William who was ten at the wedding of Charles and Isobel Grewer. The Glenisla schoolmaster James McKenzie recently married to Elizabeth Guthrie (soon to have a family himself) could well have been there too. All of which bears out the somewhat hard-to-prove-for-sure fact that marriages at this time tended to produce five to seven children.

The commonly held idea of this era is that women had vast numbers of children most of whom died. This was certainly the impression given by the famous, and it has to be acknowledged, observant, Adam Smith when he wrote about the highlands in the 1770s:

"Poverty, though it no doubt discourages, does not always prevent marriage. It seems even to be favourable to generation. A half-starved Highland woman frequently bears more than twenty children while a pampered fine lady is often incapable of bearing any.....But poverty is extremely unfavourable to the rearing of children. It is not uncommon, I have frequently been told, in the Highlands of Scotland for a mother who has borne twenty children not to have two alive."[48]

In fact the 1790 statistical report speaks of the contentment and health of the residents of Glenisla. According to this same report during the previous thirty five years children had a one in twenty chance of living past their tenth birthday. They were most likely to die under five years, but many obviously lived on. If one in twenty died, and if each family had say six children, then out of the three families we are interested in we

---

[48] Adam Smith, Wealth of Nations Everyman ed. London 1910 p70, one of the most influential economic works of the era.

could expect just one child not to reach his or her tenth birthday.

These children would have been told the local legends of Glenisla. How there was a giant, Colly Camb and his wife Smoutachantay, who lived in a cave in Mount Blair on the far side of the Isla higher up the Glen. A traveller once called the wife: Smoutachantay, Smoutachantay, what are ye doin' the day? And she replied: Makin' the porridge an lickin the theevil,[49] come in an' see. Which the traveller unwisely did , never to come out again.

Then there was the spirit child which many swore to have encountered but when met on these isolated highland paths the conversation would go -What are ye doin' here, Puddle-the-gutters? And the child would reply: I'll gae hame, I'll gae hame. Puddle-the-gutters is my name. After which it would disappear.

There was an old ballad which ran -

I'll be lost in Isla water
I'll be found in Isla stream
Bonny Bawby's me forgotten
Man an horse she's sent nae none.

This was in reference to two lovers who lived on opposite sides of the river Isla and the young man thought he had been sent a horse to get across to meet his sweetheart, but it was a hoax and he drowned. For there was a Kelpie in the shape of a docile horse who would appear to folk who were by the side of the river hoping to get across. There being no bridges in the beginning crossing the river was by foot or by horseback and

---

[49] a wooden porridge stirrer

drowning accidents were not uncommon. The kelpie would appear by a ford and the pedestrian, glad of a lift would mount, but just where the current was strong and deep the Kelpi would melt away leaving his rider to die a watery death.

Even in 1790 there were only two bridges across the Isla, one a few miles up river from the Kirk at Forter (and this had not been built until 1759) and the other nine miles downstream. This and the absence of roads on which four wheeled carts could get in to Glenisla kept it an isolated part of the country. To a traveller the Glenisla women may have appeared impoverished - not for them the tightly wasted long gowns with billowing skirts and low necklines, the richly coloured and woven patterned materials, the various hats and elegant gloves. Nor for that matter did their husbands wear the long haired wigs, the stockings and silver buckled shoes embroidered waist coats and flowing jackets over knee length britches which the Edinburgh men sported.

Inside the Craighead homes still the bare necessities with the peat fire for warmth and the homemade candles for light, again a contrast to a middle class townsman with furnished homes lit by bigger glass windows. There had been a change too in the larger land owners' home life. The previous century the "domestic furnishings of the typical lairds house were simple in the extreme" . One of the effects of the parliamentary union with England in 1707 had been to take many of the Laird class to England for long or short durations and here they would become familiar with a far more sophisticated style of living. During the eighteenth century mahogany furnishings based on designs by Chippendale, Sheraton and Hepplewhite, framed paintings, fabrics, plastered ceilings and such luxuries found their way in to the Lairds' homes. All of which had to be paid for so this brought pressure in for them to gain more cash income from their estates. There were plenty of books and pamphlets published encouraging them to increase the rents on their land by using the new Improved farming methods.

The aftermath of the '45 was further incentive for change. The Ogilvy landlords had had to seek refuge on the continent. The managers of their estates were talking farm Improvements, certainly the government meant to eradicate any further Jacobite uprisings. This meant abolishing any remaining tenancy agreements which could give a landlord power to call his men to fight for him. Encouraging the new farming methods effectively did this by reducing the number of tenants and having tenants who paid with money and not "in kind", either in goods or services.

Cortachy Castle, home of Earl of Airlie chief of Clan Ogilvy, known as "the bonnie hoose of Airlie".

The era had passed where it could be worth the Laird having a large number of men at his disposal for fighting purposes, or as a reserve labour force on their home farms. Further more the

Barony courts were abolished after Culloden so the days when the Laird exercised a paternal judiciary power over his tenants had also gone. The relationship became one which we today are more familiar with whereby a tenant paid a certain amount of money for tenure for a set period.

Significantly after 1745 the Landlords consolidated their right to kill any game in the area. This was contested by tenants who found they were not allowed to kill the odd hare, duck, deer, partridge or rabbit[50] to augment their diet. Why should the landlord have this right when the animals were wild, free to roam and could for example be on the public roadway? Yet the renting of these rights to rich folk from the south was an increasing reality over the following century.

A curious law at this time was the one regarding the ownership of bees. If the bees left a hive and were swarming, so long as the previous owner kept these swarming bees in sight they remained his; if, however he lost sight of the bees and they lodged on the property of another they became the property of the other!

Change did come to Glenisla, and probably rapidly so from 1770 to 1790. Between 1755 and 1790 there was a forty five per cent decrease in the population of the Parish of Glenisla. In 1755 the populations was said by Dr Webster to be 1,852, thirty eight years later in the statistical account of 1790 it was given as 1,018.

---

[50]The rabbits were not in Scotland in any number until later in the 19th century and were introduced much as they were in to New Zealand without realising what a pest they were to become. References to wild rabbits start after 1820 whereas they had been established in England for a long time.

Many of Charles Grewer's school mates must have left the Glen. According to the Rev James Watt, who looked back on this phenomena from 1842, it was "a decrease [which] may, in a great measure, be attributed to the converting of several contiguous pendicles of land into one possession a practice which has been occasionally adopted since the middle of the last century; and more especially to the abolition of townships by the assignation of the allotments of each to one or two separate tenants."[51]

The "contiguous pendicles" were small adjacent pieces of land which had been let out to separate families but which were regarded as being subsidiaries of larger estates. The townships were those like Craighead which were not towns as we think of them but rather a group of farmers working as a commune. William Roy's military survey map of 1747/55 show five buildings at Craighead and five at Craigniety which seem to indicate several families living in each location. In Thomson and Williams map of 1820 there are just single squares for each place plus between a square labelled "cotes", possibly sheep cotes or stone walled sheep yards.

A forty five per cent loss in population[52] could be termed a clearance, a term which if mentioned in the same sentence as Scotland has sent red lights flashing in many people's minds. Thousands of Scots who were cleared from their subsistence crofts were unwilling immigrants to the new world whilst others ended their days in severely straightened circumstances. The infamous Strathnaver clearance typifies this situation: "The consternation and confusion were extreme. Little or no

---

[51] Statistical Account 1842 pg 428-9

[52] If the population dates of 1755 and 1801 are compared there is actually a 54% loss.

time was given for the removal of persons or property; the people striving to remove the sick and the helpless before the fire should reach them; next, struggling to save the most valuable of their effects. The cries of the women and children, the roaring of the affrighted cattle, hunted at the same time by the yelling dogs of the shepherds amid the smoke and fire, altogether presented a scene that completely baffled description , it required to be seen to be believed." [53] This written by a native witness, Donald MacLeod of the time when the estate factor set fire to the homes of the crofters to enforce their departure for the land owner, the Duke of Stafford.

From the factors point of view the event was recorded thus "Lord and Lady Stafford were pleased humanely to order the new arrangement of this country. That the interior should be possessed by Cheviot shepherds, and the people brought down to the coast ……..a most benevolent action, to put these barbarous Highlanders into a position where they could better associate together, apply themselves to industry, educate their children and advance in civilisation." Which the Highlanders themselves might have come round to accepting except that not only was their displacement managed in an inhumane way but that where they were moved did not provide them with an adequate living, in fact it left them destitute.

An illustration of the harsh methods in which much of the Scottish country side was denuded of people for the placement of animals is that of the Earl of Selkirk who "went personally to the district, allured many of the evicted people to emigrate to his estates on the red River in British North America, whither a whole ship-cargo of them went. After a long and otherwise

---

[53] this in 1814 see www.undiscoveredscotland.co.uk/betty hill/strathnaver/index.html

disastrous passage, they found themselves deceived and deserted by the Earl, left to their unhappy fate in an inclement wilderness. They were without any protection from the hordes of red Indian savages by whom the district was infested, and who plundered them of their all on their arrival and finally massacred them. A small remnant who managed to escape travelled forests to upper Canada."[54]

The crofters who left Glenisla were part of a "silent clearance" meaning that there were no reports of protests or cases in the sheriff courts relating to unfair expulsions. The folk who left were probably lured as much as pushed from their homes. In the lowlands there was an increasing amount of work available - roads, bridges, and buildings required huge amounts of human labour, as did the improved farms. Sowing, reaping, weeding, gathering, managing the plough and the horses were still all labour intensive, it was just that the farm managers now hired the help they needed, a system that gave them a lot more control over their workers.

Another feature making it easier for Glenisla folk to migrate elsewhere was their language. Unlike those living in the Western and Northern Highlands they spoke English or at least Scots as distinct from the Gaelic. They also lived within walking distance of the Lothians where so many changes were taking place at this time. Then there was the English army's proud Scottish regiments which recruited substantial numbers of young men, (to fight for example for England in the American war of Independence 1775-83).

There is no mention of ruined cottar dwellings in the 1790

---

[54] www.electricscotland.com/history/

statistical analysis of Glenisla . In Liberton it was said "the ruins of demolished cottages are to be seen in every corner." They were probably there though for an 1801 survey there were 221 inhabited houses and 104 uninhabited, which is 32 percent of the total……..and if one imagined nearly a third of the houses in the parish you lived in being empty it is a remarkable situation. "Great tacks o' laun can noo be seen, whaur crofters ance dwelt snug an' bien."[55]

The following tally in 1811 noted just two uninhabited homes from a total of 231. The farm cottages did not last long once vacated. The stones would have been used to form walls, or with turf, dykes, to enclose fields. There was also a fear that vagrants and "sturdy beggars" would be attracted to any vacant cottar dwellings thus bringing a burden on to the parish. Farmers were therefore encouraged to totally demolish any uninhabited buildings.

In Craighead it appears that a stone sheep fold was made close to where dwellings had been. One two story house remained which, judging by the abandoned bath and toilet was not abandoned until the 20th century whilst the remnants of much older buildings behind it had probably been used for cattle or farm barns.

In the short term it is not clear whether the land owners made much money from the reduction in the cottar population in Glenisla. There do not seem to have been many changes in the subsistence farming methods until after 1790. Nor does there appear to have been much money being used. This is illustrated in the Sunday collections which the poor fund of the Parish

---

[55] D. Thomson, 1881, Musings from "crofters" Dictionary Scots Language.

depended upon. In 1705 these totalled only three pence a week or thirteen shillings a year; by 1790 the Sunday collection had increased but only to average three shillings and six pence a week, or nine pounds a year. The poor relief fund by then was just twelve pounds a year (the difference being made up by "charitable and well disposed persons". It still suggests that there was not a lot of cash flowing round Glenisla.

Another indication of the slowness of a money economy to come in is the story of the parish mort cloth. In 1748 there are lengthy discussions during the Kirk sessions on the purchase of a Mort Cloth (a cloth to cover the corpse at a funeral). The elder David Ogilvy reported that "he had taken out of the box £73.16s. Scots buying of the mort cloth....from Edinburgh"[56]. The main two expenses were 7 ½ yards of black hair plush, £37.10s, and a black mohair fringe, £16 18s. The making of it was only 9 pence! To recoup the money the session agreed to charge £1 Scots within the parish. There were other charges when , as often happened, a body was carried to another parish to be buried. Unfortunately folk did not make use of it so a year later it was agreed to reduce the cost to one shilling sterling to the poorer sort and 18 pence to others.
Time passed and still in 1761 the mort cloth was not even gaining the simple interest on the money it had cost to have this mort cloth and selling it was considered. Then there is no mention of it until 1792 by which time it was worn out and the minister was investigating the purchase of another which would be most advantageous for the funds of the poor. So it would appear that it was finally hired out successfully but not until the later years of that century.

---

[56]The Story of Glenisla p. 151

Chapter 6
Passing Generations, Funerals and Wakes

Bright star of the morning that beamed on the brow
Of our chief of ten thousand, oh where art thou now?
The sword of our fathers is cankered with rust,
And the race of Clan Lindsay is bowed to the dust

Sometime in the latter part of the eighteenth century Margaret Lindsay the wife of John Storar later termed Storrier died. Margaret was the great grandmother of John Storrier who was to immigrate to the New World. Hers was a clan that had known glory in an earlier period of Scottish history and maybe some such song was sung as they carried her body (with or without the mort cloth) to its grave. Their son Andrew would have had support from others living near, John McKenzie and his wife Elizabeth, Charles and Isobel Grewer and Andrew and Janet Duncan. Funerals, especially for those who had lived to a good age, were a big occasion, excellently describe by John Grewer:

"Funerals were conducted in anything but a becoming manner. No sooner had death occurred than the "lyke-wake" began, for, on no account, could the corpse be left alone. A candle had to be kept burning all night, and the night wakers had to remain until relieved in the early morning. These wakes were a curious mixture of the sacred and profane, and certainly rendered the house of death anything but the house of mourning. An over indulgence in drink was largely accountable for the incongruous proceeding which took place. The earlier hours of the evening were usually spent in mirth, jest and jollity, but, at midnight, the revelers joined-or pretended to join in- the "exercise"- that is, they read a chapter from the Bible and sang a psalm. Then the mad frolics and games were participated in. Hide -and-seek was a favourite pastime, some of the hiders even ensconcing themselves in the bed where the corpse lay. There was much practical joking of a rather rough kind. Some youths would put on a large peat fire; then, going out, barred all means of egress, and blocked the chimney. Those inside were nearly suffocated by the smoke, but, to the jokers, it was the very essence of enjoyment to listen to the coughing and even vomiting. The wakes might last for three of four nights. Indeed, so much were they enjoyed, that not infrequently the death of some individual was looked forward to with impatience.

"Disgraceful scenes were also frequently witnessed at funerals. One or two messengers were to inform the people of the date of the burial and the hour of "liftin". This did not by any means imply that those invited were expected to put in an appearance at the specified hour. As a matter of fact, they came long before. In the barn were "tables"....loaded with meat, bread, cheese and unstinted quantities of whiskey. Here, for probably hours, the "mourners" sat and drank, discussing events and transacting business. The result was that many were quite drunk before the funeral lifted. There were no hearses in those days, and the coffin had to be carried to the churchyard on two spokes by relays of four men, no matter how many miles had to be traversed. If an inn had to be passed a halt was invariably made, and more liquor partake on. Thus free fights were common, while the pall-bearers were often unable to keep their feet, the coffin not infrequently being severely damaged by numerous falls..........or in one case left behind, a fact not realised until the group met the minister at the burial ground.

"On the day after the funeral many of the women in the district gathered to "tramp" the blankets of the bed on which the deceased had expired. Drink was again supplied, for these ladies were by no means abstainers, and, occasionally, sprained ankles and even broken bones resulted. Strange to say, such lavish provision of food and drink was considered to be a mark of respect for the departed. Indeed, the slightest lack of supplies was considered derogatory to the memory of the deceased."[57]

John McKenzie recalling his boyhood - "A pretty high stone wall, with long grass on its turfed top, surrounded the burial ground and through this grass we boys privately inspected the proceedings inside at a funeral. A cart usually brought the coffin , a greybeard or an anker of whiskey, with refreshments were laid on one of the elevated tombstones, and while one party took their turn digging the grave, he others refreshed themselves - and sometimes so liberally that they did not resemble mourners. When the grave was ready the coffin was placed in it and then the whole party finished the refreshments, and generally so freely that the blood of one or more boiled over about some ancient jarr, requiring fists ere all was smooth. We waited patiently till the row began, quite certain, if it was a "respectable" funeral (i.e. one where whisky was liberally provided) that a good fight would be a consequent result. And we sometimes helped to keep up the blood boiling by a clever pelt of a stone on one of the combatants - we vanishing into the jungle around."[58]

There are many tales from these early funerals - often attended by folk from ten miles or so around the crowd could be in the

---

[57] The Story of Glenisla p. 137-140
[58] Pigeon Holes of Memory, pg 60

hundreds . Writes John McKenzie again "In those times it was common for farmers an crofters to tan and often to make their own shoes. But the leather was not always A1. So, seeing such crowds of horses, each with a saddle whose flaps would make first rate shoe soles, it is asserted that no rider brought home with him that night flaps to his saddle. The small people seldom had such a chance for shoe soles."[59]

And yet another story of a drunken procession on its way to the burial ground dropping the coffin into a river and everyone walking down the river banks admiring how well it was bobbing along before someone thought to try and retrieve it.

[59] ibid p61.

Part 2

LATE EIGHTEENTH CENTURY LIFE IN RURAL FORFARSHIRE

Burn's cottage

The age Robbie Burns, the Napoleonic wars, isolated Glen Isla at the end of the 18th century, whiskey and the smuggling trade....

John and Jane Storrier emigrated to the New World in the mid nineteenth century; their **grandparents** lived in the rural parishes of Glen Isla and Lintrathen in the late 18th century

The grandparents:

Andrew Storrier (Storar) married Margaret Grewar in **1773**

William McKenzie who married Margaret Barnet in **1776**

Elspeth Storrier who married John Duncan in **1796**

Robert Farquharson who married Jean Low in **1805**

Chapter 1

The age of Robbie Burns

In the year 1790 Sir John Sinclair gave us a nationwide picture of life throughout Scotland by his Statistical Analysis. Every Parish had to return a comprehensive report - history, geography, geology, population, agricultural practices and so on were all to be covered. Usually they were written by the resident Minister of the parish although in the case of Lintrathen an outsider, "A friend to Statistical inquiries", came in and wrote the report. His conclusions were less than enthusiastic: a village, he says, composed of "despicable huts" and a parish where the tenancy arrangements were "a disgraceful remain of a system humiliating to man"[60]. In Glenisla, the Reverend Mr James Donald, while acknowledging that his parish is wayward when it comes to the Improved agricultural systems does have an appreciation of the benefits of their life style:

"The air is very pure, and the people in general very healthy. The healthiness of the people, however, may be ascribed to their manner of living. They are not pent up in houses, nor employed in sedentary occupations like many others, but roam at large in the open air, tending flocks of sheep and cattle."[61]

From the Grewer household Charles' eldest daughter Margaret was to marry young as her father had done. Margaret is practically the same age as the famous Robert Burns; he like Margaret, came from a small tenant farming background and as

---

[60] Stat. report p 565

[61] ibid p391

he has left us such a rich word picture of his times we can have some idea of what it was like to be young in the latter part of the eighteenth century. Robbie Burns was 15 when he first fell in love. He was already working as a ploughman and it was with a girl he met on the harvest field. "Courtships occupied an important place in rustic life. While older folk were snoring the snores of the weary in their box beds, youths carrying their shoes in their hands, would creep stealthily out, and hie off to the abodes of their charmers. Then there would come the well known inviting whistle, the tap on the window pane, and the damsel, hastily attired, would step forth cautiously at the "chappin' oot" and among the sheaves in the harvest field or the less romantic, more odorous shelter of a byre, the swains cooed their rural loves."[62] It was maybe thus that twenty five year old Andrew Storrier in Craigniety wooed fifteen year old Margaret Grewer.

Or perhaps it was at one of the "rockings" when " neighbors met at each others houses, each girl bringing her spinning wheel as her mother in the olden days had brought her distaff or "rock" (from which these meetings kept their name); and there they talked and sang and laughed and flirted as the wheels whirled around; and all was brought to a close by the delicious convoying home, youths carrying gallantly the wheel of the favourite of the time through the fields when "corn rigs were bonnie" in the moonlight."

Another couple to marry from Craighead in these years was William McKenzie and Margaret Barnet in 1776. Perhaps at this wedding the groom and maybe some guests would be wearing the tartan. This custom had been forbidden by the

---

[62] Scottish Men of Letters in the eighteenth Century, Henry Grey Graham. pg 384/5

English government after the defeat of Bonnie Prince Charlie in 1746. We know from Robbie Burns that the tartan was being worn again because it was said that at the Kirk on Sundays, Robbie, the handsomest and gayest of all, would wear his plaid around his shoulders in a manner of his own..........Perhaps William and Margaret had courted at the Kirk? Robbie for his part between the sermons went with the lassies to stroll the fields while the seniors went to the inn.

It was a generation which did not take the puritanical disciplines of the church quite as seriously as their parents. Burn's songs and poems were not always appreciated by the elders. "What he (Burns) wrote for his friends delectation was what the hinds [young women] were saying at the farm. They would appear demurely before the minister and congregation to express their penitence and to receive rebuke, and then go back to the farm yard and laugh over it all; men and women joining in loud guffaws over the elders, the minister and the offenders".[63]

In Alyth in 1761 the Kirk stool was no longer used - but perhaps the congregation were more able to pay the fines which replaced the stool. In Glenisla John Gilloch was paid £3.12s. Scots for a new stool of repentance in 1764, so it was still in use. But even there strong objections were being made and in that same year two offenders offered to pay rather than "sit on the common seat of repentance" and the session found that "each of the two named persons may sit in any seat they please, only they must appear publicly to be rebuked upon their paying £13 Scots to the poor, each one for themselves."[64]

---

[63] ibid 387
[64] The Story of Glenisla 142

This could well have been a case of fornication, or, as it was much more delightfully termed in Scots,   hoch or hough-magandie:

> The priest convenes his scandal court,
> Tae ken what hough-magandie sport
> Has been gaun on within the parish[65]

It was obviously a sport on which Burns and his friends held a different view on to those of the church elders. A Robert Tamahill wrote

> Be not sair on hough-magandie
> As it's a fit o' friendly passion,
> And vera muckle now in fashion.[66]

The type of charges which might be drawn up by the elders were not always to do with illicit relationships. A Mr Hamilton was charged of being an irregular attendant in church and negligent of his family worship, he was also said to have directed his gardener to dig potatoes on the lords day, to be heard whistling on a Fast Day and even to say damn it before the Ministers very face.

Religion was a much discussed topic. Not everyone necessarily believed as the epitaph Robbie Burns was to write for his beloved school teacher implied some agnostic inclinations in this respected man:

> An honest man here lies at rest
> As e'er God with his image blest!
> The friend of man, the friend of truth

---

[65] Dict. Scots Language, R. Tamahill, Poems 1896

[66] ibid, Poems, J. Lauderdale 1796

The friend of age, and guide of youth:
Few hearts like his, with virtue warm'd
Few heads with knowledge so inform'd:
If there's another world, he lives in bliss;
If there's none, he made the best of this.

Robbie himself would discuss theology in the Kirk yard "sometimes from sheer perversity taking up the Calvinistic side and at others flaunting his wilder notions".[67] It was, said Burns, odd that the sheep should choose the shepherd, but that was how it was in the church of Scotland . It was probably this democratic character that made religion such a discussed topic - National church synods held in Edinburgh would draw crowds and Broadsheets (one sided notices) would distribute information on them throughout the country.

The Calvinistic religion which fuelled dramatic "three mile" (very long) sermons and "two mile" prayers promulgated ideas like original sin: mankind was born sinful and only by the freely given "grace" of God could one escape fire and brimstone and the bottomless pit. The proof that you were one of the lucky elect and a recipient of Gods Grace was that you had faith . It followed that if you had faith you would not sin, hence the importance to communities that its members remained on the straight and narrow. It was however a code of predestination: it was the grace of God and not your actions that brought you into the elect group of believers.

These ideas were challenged by those who believed that man had an ability to discern good from bad actions and that mankind had the ability, the free will, to choose the path he took. These thinkers dwelt more on the beauty of human nature

---

[67] Scottish Men of Letters in the 18th Century, Grey Graham, p386

and the benevolence of God. It was one of the moderates, Scottish Professor Hutcheson who wrote the phrase that Jeremy Bentham was to become famous for and which many today, albeit unconsciously, take as a basis for deciding what is good and bad: "that that action is best which procures the greatest happiness of the greatest number".

Did our farmers in the Glens bother about such notions? No doubt this depended on the individual. What was likely was that the households would have been assembled in the evenings and the father would begin with the solemn words "Let us worship God" and would read a portion of the "word of God". The ability to read was widespread (more so than the ability to write). Homes with the scantiest of furnishings would contain a bible and many "hovels" contained surprisingly literary books. You might find copies of such works by Shakespeare, or books such as Taylor's "On Original Sin", Stockhouse's "History of the Bible", Ramsay's Poems, John Locke "On the Human Understanding", and if the household was inclined collections of ballads and songs.

The Storriers one assumes came from a line of shepherds, Andrew's father John was called Storar, someone who herded the sheep. And here is an account by an nineteenth century shepherd, albeit an English not a Scottish one, on the part the Bible could play in a shepherds life: "Caleb and his brothers had been taught their letters when small, and the Bible was their one book, which they read not only in the evenings at home but during the day when they were with the flock. His extreme familiarity with the whole Scripture narrative was a marvel to me.....there is that in the old Scriptures which appeals in a special way to the solitary man who feeds his flock....I remember well in the days of my boyhood and youth, when living in a purely pastoral country. ....how

88

understandable and eloquent many of the ancient stories were to me. The life, the outlook, the rude customs and the vivid faith in the Unseen............"[68]

For the most part however it is likely that Elizabeth Grant's summation was accurate enough for the early 19th century: "there was no very deep religious feeling in the Highlands ....the established form of faith was determinately adhered to, but the "kittle questions", which had so vexed the Puritanical south, had not yet troubled the minds of their northern neighbours. Our mountains were full of fairy legends, old clan tales, forebodings, prophecies, and other superstitions, quite as much believed in as the Bible. The Shorter Catechism and the fairy stories were mixed up together to form the innermost faith of the Highlander, a much gayer and less metaphysical character than his Saxon tainted countryman."[69]

This tradition of strong Christian faith intermingled with a love of fairies was one which later went out to the colonies . On mossy banks beneath ferns and by chattering rivers children were shown the fairies' homes and would have recognised instantly the folk "of small stature, but finely proportioned, of a fair complexion, with long yellow hair handing over their shoulders and gathered above their heads with combs of gold. They wore a mantle of green cloth, inlaid with wild flowers; green pantaloons, buttoned with bobs of silk, and silver shoon.....they ride steeds whose hoofs would na dash the dew from the cup of a harebell........"[70]

---

[68] A Shepherds Life W H Hudson

[69] Memoirs of a Highland Lady 1797-1827, Elizabeth Grant

[70] The Silver Bough. Scottish Folk lore and Folk Belief, F.M. McNeill p111 Edin 1989

During the nineteenth century people began to view society in terms of "class". During the eighteenth century the class differences, which were to be the anathema of colonial people, became apparent to more folk in Scotland. Previously there had been a small aristocracy but even the Lairds lived in a rudimentary fashion and indeed they had a system of fostering out their sons to another family within the clan such that they grew up very much one of the people.

This similarity in life styles can be seen in the description of the home of Thomas Ogilvie of Eastmiln. He called himself a Laird and his wife a Lady. Yet the house was humble enough, it isdescribed here in 1766 when Katherine Nairn (20) was accused of poisoning her old husband Thomas Ogilvy (41) because she was in love with the younger brother, Lieutenant Patrick Ogilvy:

: "...the house consisted of two story's; upon the ground floor there were but two rooms, kitchen and parlour, one on either side of the entrance hall or passage; on the flat above were two bedrooms corresponding to the rooms below. A garret roof was used as a store-room. We learn from the evidence that the servants slept in the kitchen, beneath the west bed-room occupied by the laird and his wife; that the east bedroom, above the parlour, was assigned to the lieutenant; and that Anne Clark and old Lady Eastmiln shared a box-bed in the parlour...a family of five persons and three servants were thus accommodated in four small rooms."[71]

---

[71] Twelve Scots Trials, William Roughead 1913. This was the same Ogilvy family which had caused the dismissal of the Minister in Glenisla in 1740. At the time the latter had predicted that none of the Eastmiln men " would not die the death common to men". This prediction came true. One had fallen from the Edinburgh castle trying to escape after the '45. Thomas was probably poisoned with arsenic. Patrick was accused of this and hung. His younger brother (who *could* have been the accomplice to the maid who

By the end of the eighteenth century there are wider divisions amongst the Scots in their comparative wealth and ways of life: Lairds who live the high life in London, agricultural labourers who no longer have a plot of land to work for themselves, well to do farmers are becoming established in the lowlands, while the towns are growing and with this the haves and the have-nots.

Robbie Burns was one to feel the sting of class distinction as he wrote in his diary how it galled him to see Lord Glencairn pay deference to a man of higher station : " He showed so much engrossing attention to the only blockhead at the table that I was within half a point of throwing down my gage of contemptuous defiance. It was mortifying to see a fellow whose abilities would scarcely have made a eight penny tailor, and whose heart is not worth three farthings, meet with the attention and notice that are withheld from the son of genius and poverty".

Burns wrote in the vernacular Scots language and in his day he had his critics . Gentlemen were known to raise their eyebrows under their capacious wigs or powdered hair and refer to him as that illiterate ploughman. But as Graham points out "had he [Burns] been born forty years earlier when town and country manners were more alike, when classes high and low had less difference in living, when laird and merchant, lawyer and shopkeeper were of kindred blood, all speaking broad Scots, all with frugal incomes and simple ways........the disparity of rank

---

could have done the murder!) was later accused of bigamy and then fell from a high window in Edinburgh while watching a procession.. Katherine actually escaped from prison disguised as a midwife, her fate after that unknown, although the child she had carried throughout the trial died after two months.

and manners ....would have been less marked between Ayrshire farmer and Edinburgh citizen."[72]

[72] Scottish Men of Letters op cit p401

Chapter 2

The Napoleonic Wars[73]

The chances of a healthy Highland Scotsman being called up between 1793 and 1815 were high: an estimated seventy four thousand men, a quarter of the regional population of three hundred thousand were drafted.[74]With the consolidation of farms there were fewer tenant farmers and many young men who were not attached to a particular piece of land but who moved around working as agricultural labourers or servants. They were not permanently attached to a piece of land and they could be picked up by recruitment sergeants arriving in market towns with the bagpipes, whisky and the offer of a bounty payment.

Recruitments for "regiments of the line" could be for the Fencibles[75], the Volunteers[76] or the Militia. Regiments of the line were foot soldiers which stood in line on the battlefields contrasting to the Light Infantry which had been developed during the American Wars and whose soldiers carried far less

---

[73] *The Storrier family living in Craigneity and the McKenzie family living in Craighead both had children who could have been called up, or have husbands called up, during the Napoleonic wars:* Andrew Storrier m 1773 Margret Grewar whose children were Elspeth b1774 , David b 1776, Margaret b 1782 Charles b 1785 and Jean b1787. William McKenzie m1776 Margaret Barnet and their family - Martha b 1777 William b1780 Janet b 1781 Agnes b1784 Jean b1787 Susan b 1793 John b1789

[74] Whateley, Scottish Society 1707-1830 pg 251. And Devine in The Scottish Nation p 185

[75] Fencible may have come from "defensible", in any event it referred to a Defensive unit.

[76] Citizen units

being equipped rather to scout and skirmish.

After 1745 the local militias had been outlawed but the threat of Napoleon invading changed this. Wrote Lord Cockburn "...thinking men were in a great and genuine fright, which increased as they thought. The apparent magic of Napoleon's Continental success confounded them. Ireland made them shudder; and they saw that a war in this thick-set and complicated country , however short and triumphant, must give a dreadful shock to our whole system."[77]

In 1794 the Angusshire Regiment of Fencible Infantry was embodied, as it was called when the men were gathered. Their commander was Colonel Archibald Douglas. In this regiment was Colonel Charles Hunter a landowner whose Burnside property stretched from near Kiriemuir to the Firth of Tay below Dundee. They are recorded as having been equipped with the blue scot's bonnets and Highland Trews (diamond patterned footed stockings) as their uniform. This was in comparison with say the Argyllshire Regiment who were issued with full Highland dress including the kilt, belted plaid, hose, bonnet, shoes and great coat.[78]

David Storrier (John Storrier's father) was 18 when this regiment was formed and 26 when it was disbanded in 1802. Perhaps this explained why he did not marry until 1809 when

---

[77] Memorials of His Time , Lord Cockburn pg119

[78] Trews were normally worn by those who could afford to ride a horse so it seems unlikely that the private foot soldiers recruited would have worn these. The Lowland regiments actually wore the British uniform. The Angus shire regiment was not listed amongst the 18 Highland regiments but as one of the Lowland ones, yet they obviously were akin to the former as they were issued bonnets and trews. This was the closest embodiment of regiments to Glenisla hence the description entered in to here.

he was thirty three. Whilst the Angus shire Regiment was not raised in Glenisla David was at the age when he would likely have left home to find agricultural work elsewhere. This Regiment served in Ireland. They were there in a defensive role as it was feared Napoleon would attack England through Ireland and indeed in 1789 500 ships with 15,000 men left Brest for Bantry Bay, but a wind created havoc and the French army returned without having landed.

The French were to have liaised with the United Irishmen, a group rebelling against the English rule which consisted of Dissenters, Catholics and Protestants. They continued to cause the British some trouble, the height of their campaign being when they took control of Enniscorthy having dispersed the defence by stampeding cattle through the town. Whether or not the Angus shire regiment was involved is uncertain but the time involved bloodshed and a blind eye was turned to what was described as military excesses.

Originally these regiments like the Angus shire had a Colonel, a Lieutenant Colonel, a Lieutenant, a Major, 5 Captains, an ensign, 3 Sergeants, 4 Corporals, 2 Drummers and 71 Privates. Joining the army was a way of improving ones status and the more men a property owner could bring with him the better for him. To begin with there was a uniform and a bounty, which seems to vary from three to twenty guineas. This Angus shire Regiment was part of what is now called The Forgotten Army since these were regiments that were largely disbanded with the Peace of Amiens in 1802 which briefly ceased the fighting between England and Napoleon. They are "Forgotten" since all the focus thereafter tended to be on Waterloo.

Many of these regiments and all the volunteer corps stayed in Scotland as a defense force for invasion so that the Regular army were freed to be sent abroad. It would seem that the volunteer army was somewhat inefficient. "Don't let the awkward squad fire over me", Robbie Burns is purported to have said on his deathbed in 1796 referring to his fellow soldiers in the volunteer corps. Lord Cockburn as a young man was "a gallant captain, commanding ninety-two of my fellow creatures from 1804 to 1814" being part of the Midlothian Volunteers and says of these Volunteer battalions " for the ...service for which it was intended they should be prepared, they were totally disqualified. They had no field equipage, and were scarcely ever trained to march beyond their parade ground Certainly no volunteer regiment in Scotland ever passed twenty-four hours at a time, in the open air, upon its own resources..."[79]

"When we first began" relates Cockburn, "being resolved that we townsmen should outshine the rustic, we actually drilled our two companies almost every night during the four winter months of 1804 and 1805, by torchlight....The parades, the reviews, the four or six yearly inspections....the mock battles, the marches, the messes - what scenes they were! And similar scenes were familiar in every town and in every shire in the kingdom. The terror of the ballot for the regular militia which made those it hit soldiers during the war, filled the ranks; while duty, necessity, and especially the contagion of the times, supplied officers. The result was that we became a military population. Any able-bodied man, of whatever rank, who was not a volunteer, or a local militia man, had to explain or apologise for his singularity."

This being the state of the nation it is likely that the young Glenisla men would have been touched in some way by the

---

[79] Memorials of his Time, Lord Cockburn p 118

war. David's younger brother Charles was nineteen in 1800, when nineteen to twenty three year olds were being targeted by the ballot. David's future wife Janet had a brother William who was nineteen in 1799 - if he did serve he returned alive as he married David's sister Jean Storrier in 1810.

Of the volunteers Cockburn thought that the joining " tended to unsettle the minds of those who belonged to them for ordinary business; and hence they co-operated with the ballot in filling the ranks of the militia, which was the great nursery of the army. In this way the voluntary establishments were a very useful force; and if they had been called into active service, all the paid regiments, that is, all those composed of hardy ploughmen and artisans, would have soon become good practical soldiers."[80] The fighting resumed after the failure of the Peace of Amiens and continued until the Battle of Waterloo in 1815.

Spring comes to Kirrie, all the world's in bloom
Winter is forgiven now, fooled by April's bloom,
Kirrie, oh Kirrie, you were ae my hame
Till Napoleon's bloody cannon hit their aim.
The cold returns in Autumn
When the wind rakes the trees
And the summer lies forgotten
In a cold bed of leaves
As winter begins aye mind Boney
It wasn't only you
Who was broken on the field of Waterloo

Jeanie oh Jeanie I am surely done

---

[80] ibid p 120

Stricken down in battle, at the mouth o Boney's guns,
Jeanie oh Jeanie, aye sae dear to me,
Let me hold you in my mind afore I dee.
For the cold....

Surgeon oh surgeon, leave me wi my pain
Save you knife for others, who will surely rise again,
Surgeon oh surgeon, leave my blood to pour,
Let it drain into the bitter clay once again.
For the cold...

Daughter oh daughter, listen tai me
Never wed a sodger, or a widow you will be
Daughter oh daughter, curse your lad to die,
Ere he catches the recruiting sergeants eye,
For the cold....

Boney oh Boney, war was aye your game,
Bloody field your table, canon yours to aim,
Boney oh Boney, we aye lived the same,
Drilling laddies not to fear the muskets flame,
For the cold returns in autumn
When the wind rakes the trees
And the summer lies forgotten
In a cold bed of leaves
As winter begins aye mind Boney
It wasn't only you
Who was broken on the field of Waterloo.

This modern ballad[81] is written about a soldier who left
Kirriemuir to fight for King and country and was slain on the
Waterloo battle field. He did well to turn down the surgeon's

---

[81]   Jim Malcolm, Scottish folksinger, 2008

help since it was not for another ninety years that a patient had more chance of living than dieing after being operated on. Some did survive the surgeons knife like Alexander MacKenzie who "in the course of his service was dangerously wounded in the neck, lost an eye, and had two horses killed under him. He was a gallant and distinguished officer, in every sense a thorough Highlander."[82] One who was not saved was Lieutenant Farquharson who was "shot is in the back by a Spanish sentry".[83] This being particularly unfortunate since at this stage the Spanish were fighting with the English against the French. The soldiers who did fight in Europe were actually more likely to die of cholera, typhoid and other diseases than from the battlefield.

The rural highlanders in the regular army could have ended up in many a far off land - European countries through to Egypt. Those in the Navy in the Atlantic or through the Mediterranean. The Navy was another area which absorbed many Scots, willing and unwilling recruits from seaside towns. This was a time when press gangs operated but they were after seafarers, only rarely were non-seamen impressed. At one stage early in the 19th century the Navy was intercepting immigrant ships to impress all the those able bodied men who were hoping for a new start across the Atlantic. The capture of American sailors for British warships was one of the reasons America went to war with the British Empire between 1812 and 1814.

General Ogilvy from Inverquarity Castle in the Angus Glens served at sea in the Napoleonic wars and it is possible that he

---

[82] www.electricscotland.com/history/scotreg/mcculloch/story4.htm

[83] A History of the Peninsular War. The biographical Dictionary of British Officers killed and Wounded 1808-1814 by John A. Hall

drew on his Farquharson contacts in Lintrathen when enlisting men. Jane Duncan's grandfather Robert Farquharson was twenty at the start of the Napoleonic wars, if he was involved he survived to return home in 1805 and marry Jean Low in the Glenisla church.

Scotland Forever!   Lady Elizabeth Butler

An aftermath of the Napoleonic war was the change in popular conception of the Highlanders. Time was, wrote Lord MacCauley in his great tombs of "The History of England" that nine Scotchmen out of ten considered the kilt to be the dress of a thief. There was a Muse's poem from the seventeenth century that encapsulated how the English and most lowlanders felt about the highlanders:

"How the first Hyndman of God was maid of Ane horse Turd
in Argyle."

Says God to the cram's "Quhair wilt thou now?
I will down to the Lowlands, Lord, and there steal a cow.
"Ffy," quod St Peter, " thou wilt never do weel,
An thou, but new made, so sure gais to steal"
"Umff" quod the hielandman, and swore by yon Kirk.
"So long as I may get geir to steal, will I nevir work."[84]

It was also observed re the massacre of the MacDonalds in
Glencoe that "no Scots or English statesmen would have
thought ordering the extirpation of a Lowland or English
community but a highland clan [that] was a different matter."

However in 1822 the chubby George IV appeared dressed in a
highland outfit - "carefully placing the fall of the kilt and plaid
about his plump Hanoverian king's pink tights", signifying the
"arrival" of the Highland dress.

The favourable change of opinion of the Highlanders which
had swept throughout Scotland and into England had been
fostered by the works of Walter Scott and Robbie Burns. It was
augmented by David Stewart of the Black Watch Regiment. In
1822 Stewart published his Sketches of the Character, Manners
and Present State of the Highlanders of Scotland. It could well
be the filtering down of his view that made it important for we
colonial offspring to find our roots not in the Lowlands but in
the Highlands of Scotland.....a close run matter in this instance
with Glenisla and Lintrathen on the very brink of the Highland
Fault.

---

[84] The History of England Lord MacCauley vol 11 p 33

Bathmodelcentre.com　　　　*British and Scots Regiments*

The Highlander, wrote Stewart, has " a hardihood which enable him to sustain severe privations. As the simplicity of his life gave vigour to his body so it fortified his mind. Possessing a frame and constitution thus hardened, he was taught to consider courage as the most honourable virtue, cowardice the most disgraceful failing; to venerate and obey his chief and to devote himself for his native country and clan; and thus prepared to be a soldier, he was ready to follow wherever honour and duty called him. With such principles, and regarding any disgrace he aught bring on his clan and district as the most cruel misfortune, the Highland private soldier has a peculiar motive to exertion. He goes into the field resolved not to disgrace his name. A strong characteristic of the Highlander, is that all his actions seem to flow from sentiment. His endurance of privation and fatigue, his resistance of hostile opposition, his solicitude for the good opinion of his superiors, all originate in this source, whence also proceeds his obedience."

Chapter 3

An Isolated Glen

The poor state of the roads did not facilitate change in Glenisla where in 1790 "the roads are in very bad repair, and must continue in the same state till proper overseers are appointed to inspect them, and road money of the parish appropriated to their repair."[85] To Adam Smith the poor state of repair was in part due to organisation but it was not a problem he wished cured in the manner of the French where "the exactions are frequently the most cruel and oppressive. Such *corvees* as they are called, make one of the principle instruments of tyranny by which those officers chastise any parish or *communaute* which has the misfortune to fall under their displeasure."[86] Whereas, he says, in Great Britain "under the local or provincial administration the six days' labour which the country people are obliged to give to the reparation of the highways is not always perhaps very judiciously applied, but it is scarce ever exacted with any circumstances of cruelty or oppression."

John McKenzies impressions as a young man of the Scottish road workers in the first half of the nineteenth century were that the men enjoyed their sixty hours per year which the rent of their places entailed. He noted that the amount of alcohol consumed and the comradeship seemed to make it a convivial time, at least in his area on the west coast.

The turn-pike roads built with tolls to pay to cover the costs

---

[85] stat anal p 395

[86] Wealth of Nations vol 2 p219

which were criss-crossing the lowlands were not developed in Glenisla and the four mile route out to Alyth and the eight miles to Kirriemuir both had hills to negotiate which were particularly difficult in winter. There was a coach which ran from Edinburgh to Aberdeen in 1798 which carried post and three passengers, an armed guard for fear of French soldiers, and men attended to render assistance when soft ground had to be negotiated. It took fourteen hours for this journey which included regular four minute halts to change the four horses. During the Napoleonic wars horses were dearer as they had been taken for cavalry, corn and hay prices increased. Still there was a demand for these coaches as letters and papers with news of the war were carried by them. Post was paid for on arrival per sheet, and there were constant complaints at this time of its tardiness, especially letters for London which seemed to get held up in Edinburgh.

Amongst those who were not impressed by Scottish roads was Robbie Burns who wrote an "Epigram on Rough Roads -
I'm now arrived thanks to the gods! -Thro' pathways rough and muddy
A certain sign that makin roads is not this peoples study:
Altho' I'm not wi' scriptures cram'd
I'm sure the bible says
That heedless sinners shall be damn'd
Unless they mend their ways."

Living in this isolated Glen at this time was Andrew Storrier, Jane Duncan's great grandfather, he was also the grandfather of her husband John Storrier. Lives entwined in the small and still static society of the Forfarshire Glens. This Andrew Storrier married Margaret Grewer. Andrew Storrier and Margaret Grewer (women were often referred to by their maiden names even after marriage) had five children at Craigneity. The eldest two both married in to families from Craighead: Elspeth married John of the Duncan family while David married Janet, known as Jessie, McKenzie.

Departure of the Scottish Bride

John Duncan of Craighead married Elspeth Storrier of Craigneity in 1796. They continued to live in Craighead possibly in the same dwelling that John's father and mother, Andrew and Janet had gone to when they married in 1740. By 1796 the population of Glenisla had significantly reduced and some remaining tenants had improved their homes. The animals may now have been in a separate building and the house would have two rooms, a but and a ben. The interior was little altered although the married couple and perhaps the youngest children, would sleep in a separate room, the ben, which may even have wooden floor boards. No one lives at Craighead today. There are remnants of the earlier stone and turf dwellings with a sheep pen nearby which may well have been built from their stones; further on are more substantial stone walls which may have housed this early nineteenth century family. Beside these is a two story stone walled and tiled roofed house perhaps built in the 1830's and which, containing a toilet and bath, must have been in use well into the twentieth century.

John Duncan had been the youngest of five children and had not married until he was forty one years old. Perhaps his siblings left Glenisla and he remained helping his parents. At any event it is likely that, unlike the period when young Charles Grewer married at a young age, John had to wait for a vacant tenancy. Elspeth was twenty two when they married and in the twenty years after their marriage they had ten children, all born at Craighead.

We have a good picture of the Glen at this time from the Rev. James Donald's statistical analysis report. In 1790 very little of the commonties (land held in common by a group of farmers) had been enclosed ."The greater part of the inhabitants have small farms, with considerable extent of pasturage annexed to them. About fifty four of them are small proprietors or portioners, and a great part of these occupy their lands themselves."[87]

The Kirkton of Glenisla was just a church with its manse, an inn and a school. It was not a village with rows of houses and shops. People made most of their own goods, additional requirements being bought from passing tinkers or pedlars or from visits to Alyth (the closest market town), Meigle (having the nearest Post Office), Kirriemuir, Forfar, Arbroath or

---

[87] stat. analysis p 392

Dundee. The three blacksmiths, seven tailors and four wrights (craftsmen such as mill wrights who kept the machinery in the mill going) would also have land they tilled for their own food. It would seem that the reduction in population had put more land into the hands of fewer farmers but not all the old subsistence methods had been relinquished.

In the upper part of the parish, which would include Craighead, the Scotch plough was still in use, the four or sometimes six horses yoked abreast of one another with the driver in the lead walking backwards. The horses were small highland ponies without the great strength of the English draft horses. On the lower parts of the Glen the English plough was used which had two horses and was operated by one man who was also the driver of the horses walking behind. This plough was one of the two mechanical labour saving agricultural machines that were introduced in the eighteenth century. The other device was the threshing machine invented in 1787 but whilst it quickly came into use in the lower regions the hand flail was still used in the remoter parts. James Smith recalled his experience with the flail as a young farm worker in the region in 1822 "I had to stand every morning in the barn and take my share at the flail as they called it - a tremendous work it may be useful to explain to you the manner in which this flail so called was wrought - what shape it was - first the shape was two long stilts the one a deal thicker than the other...a stick fastened with a loop of straw swung it around your head with all your might blow for blow on the corn on the floor two or three sheaves at a time...I found this flailing to be very sore for me...I might have failed but for my comrade Ian a little short fellow who was very kind to me...the work was too heavy for me...I never could get a rest because it was a daily repetition of a work which was too heavy for me. I was truly glad when this six months came to an end but I was stronger at the end."[88]

There was one "improved" farm at Kilry[89] where the heritor was "sufficiently aware of the advantages and propriety of improving ground covered with heath, has inclosed a good many acres of muir ground adjacent to his house, with fir and birch trees, which presently appear to be in a thriving state." And the Rev Donald adds " Would his neighbors follow his example the country would not wear the bleak aspect it does."[90]

Working against such improvements were the climate and the road conditions. From this same report we learn that the frost caused havoc with the crops making it unfeasible at least in the higher regions, to plant potatoes and wheat and even damaging the bere crops at times. As for turnips, another crop rotation used advantageously by the "improving" farmers, " it is impossible that this crop can turn out to advantage while the inhabitants allow their sheep to feed promiscuously after the corns are put into the barn yards."[91] It was possibly that it was this problem that had prompted the Factor in his 1781 conditions to try and enforce a set date for the sheep to go to the upland pastures.

The Rev Donald continues "With respect to animal production, the country abounds in black cattle; these are generally of a small size but very durable..........the sheep which are generally kept in the hilly part, are but of a small size; some of

---

[88] Memoirs of James Smith Stonemason Dundee 1805-c1869 pg 6

[89] I have made the assumption that this property is at Kilry as it is the only one with a plantation on Wm Roy's military map of 1747-55

[90] stat. analysis 1790 p394

[91] ibid p 395

the inhabitants, however, go yearly to the south of Scotland, where they purchase numbers of black faced sheep." In fact they went to the markets in the border towns of Linton and Lanark so it must have involved weeks of droving.

As Adam Smith pointed out the price of the cattle was one of the catalysts in the radical changes to the lives of the Highlanders. "Of all the commercial advantages, however, which Scotland has derived from the union with England, this rise in the price of cattle is, perhaps, the greatest. It has not only raised the value of all highland estates, but it has, perhaps, been the principal cause of the improvement of the low country."[92] The rise in the price of cattle would eventually "render it profitable to cultivate land for the sake of feeding them"......so gradually animals would replace people in the glens.

---

[92] Wealth of Nations vol 1 p204

Chapter 4

Whisky and the Smuggling Trade

Scottish distillery

Glenisla with no good roads in or out remained an isolated pocket on the edge of the fertile Strathmore valley. This could have been advantageous for the farmers' secondary industry: illicit whiskey making. This had been going on since the Malt tax of 1725 had made it profitable to brew and sell whiskey secretly. The profits for this business grew markedly after the government increased the tax on alcohol after 1815. (The justification for this tax was the impoverishment of the government following the war, which the English won, against Napoleon).

It was said of this time that everyone living in Glenisla was a smuggler or a smuggler's friend. The smugglers were concerned with the distillation and sale of illicit alcohol. During the Napoleonic war gentlemen had continued to drink French claret, rum and brandy but since official trade had ceased between the two countries this was being smuggled in to the west of the country and then distributed across it. The whiskey once made was transported by kegs slung across pack ponies, although women were also used, carrying it in bladders beneath voluminous skirts.

The brewing of whiskey was a way of turning the inferior quality barley grown in the highlands in to a saleable product. The landlords were not going to stop their tenants producing it as it was a way for the latter to make their rent money. The excise men were sent in to Glenisla to get the tax money but were not received kindly so they were accompanied by a small group of troopers. Still the brewers were not inclined to give in easily so there were confrontations where the soldiers' sabres were fought back by stout staves and cudgels.

The minister of the church at the time was a local supporter and he would see the excise party arrive from his manse window - his manse overlooking the public house where they stopped to refresh themselves (with a drink?) when they entered the glen. The Rev. Andrew Burns would slip away on his horse and ride in haste to all the smugglers bothie's waving his hat and shouting "The Philistines be upon thee Samson". Thus warned there would be a rush to hide the copper "head and worm" used in the distilling process and all other evidence. There were in this hilly glen with large uncultivated areas plenty of hiding places.

On one occasion though there was very little time to hide the fermenting barley so it was hurriedly placed in sacks and dumped out in a field at regular intervals to look as if it was seed ready to be planted. By such means the excise men were constantly frustrated, so much so that one day Supervisor McLeod from Coupar Angus was so mad he set a farm barn ablaze. But having found no evidence the smugglers complained bitterly to the Justice of the Peace:

"they [the gaugers or excise men] then went to a sheep cote, where they sometime before had found some smuggled stuff, and when not finding anything belonging smuggling, they went to the said sheep-cote carrying peats and heather to it, and then set it aburning, which, had it not been the goodness of providence in turning the wind from the north to the north-east our whole houses, ourselves, wives and children along with our corn and cattle being in the Dead of night, had all been burned to ashes...............so if the Fiscal of the county doth not put a stop to such Barbarous practises, Blood for Blood must be allowed."[93]

John McKenzie recalled that "Even so late as, say. 1820, one would go far ere he met a person who shrank from smuggling. My father never tasted any whisky but smuggled. [Smuggled being not just a term for illegally imported but also for the distillation of illicit whiskey.] And as every mortal that called on him (of his people, and they were legion, daily) had a dram instantly poured into him, the ankers of whiskey emptied yearly must have been legion. I don't believe he or my Mother ever dreamed that smuggling was a crime.

"In the good old times when we were going to shoot, my Mother often called our dear shooting help, gave him a tin can and desired him to bring it back filled with barm, I.e. yeast. It never occurred to her that he might not meet with a bothy,

---

[93] The Story of Glenisla p 119

brewing, ere we came home, I have been in several bothys in an ordinary day's walk and, of course, had a mug of sweet "wort", or a drop of dew (whiskey) , drank to the brewer's good luck. As in those days we baked at home, and barm from beer-makers was generally bitter from the hops used, and as my Mother and we could not stand bitter bread, what could the dear soul do but prefer barm from the smugglers? Our largest tenants , probably worth £8,000-£10,000, we always understood had made every penny by smuggling."[94]

Of these days the Free Church leader Dr Thomas Guthrie who grew up in Brechin not so far from Glenisla, wrote "Everyone, with few exceptions, drank what was in reality illicit whisky - far superior to that made under the eye of the Excise - lords and lairds, members of Parliament and Ministers of the Gospel, and everybody else... ..when a boy in Brechin, I was quite familiar with the appearance and on-goings of the Highland smugglers. They rode on Highland ponies, carrying on each side of their small, shaggy, but brave and hardy steeds, a small cask, or "keg" as it was called, of illicit whisky, manufactured amid the wilds of Aberdeenshire or the glens of the Grampians. They took up a position on some commanding eminence during the day, where they could, as from a watch-tower, descry the distant approach of the enemy, the excise man or gauger; then, when night fell, every man to horse, descending the mountains only six miles from Brechin, they scoured the plains, rattled into the villages and towns, disposing of their whisky to agents they had everywhere; and now safe, returned at their leisure, or often in a triumphal procession.

"They were often caught, no doubt, with the contraband whisky in their possession...But daring, stout, active, fellows - they often broke through the nets , and were not slack, if it

---

[94] Pigeon Holes of Memory p 304-305

offered them a chance of escape , to break the heads of the augers. I have see a troop of thirty of them riding in Indian file, and in broad day, through the streets of Brechin, after the had succeeded in disposing of their whisky, and, as they rode leisurely along, beating time with their formidable cudgels on the empty barrels to the great amusement of the public and mortification of the excise men, who had nothing for it but to bite their nails and stand, as best they could, the raillery of the smugglers and the laughter of the people...."[95]

Joseph Mitchell an engineer working on the development of highland roads recalled a scene which as he said would have been grand material for an artist: "one morning as I was driving up Glenmoriston before breakfast and taking a turn in the road of that beautiful valley, I saw before me at some little distance about twenty-five highland horses tied to each other, and carrying two kegs of whisky each. They were attended by ten or twelve men , some in kilts and all with bonnets and plaids and carrying large bludgeons. When they say me approach two of them fell back until I came up with them. They scrutinised me sharply and said, "It is a fine morning sir;" to which I responded. Then one turned to the other and said, "Ha rickh shealess ha mach Mitchel fere rate-mohr;" the literal translation of which is, "You need not mind; it is the son of Mitchell, the man of the high roads."
He then turned to me and said, "Would you took a dram?" and on my assenting he took out of his pocket a round tin snuff box, then common, but without the lid, holding about a large wine glassful, and filled it with whisky from a bottle which he took from his side pocket.
After some kindly greeting and talk and drinking my dram I passed on, the other men politely touching their bonnets as I

---

[95] ibid p309-310

left.

Almost all wines, spirits and foreign commodities supplied to the Highlands [circa 1820] were smuggled, chiefly from Holland."[96]

Due to the overall consensus in the Highlands when it came to smuggling those who were caught were "treated with greater consideration than ordinary prisoners. Their offence was not considered a heinous one, and they were not regarded as criminals. It is said that smugglers were several times allowed home from Dingwall jail for Sunday, and for some special occasions, and that they honorably returned to durance vile. Imprisonment for illicit distillation was regarded neither as a disgrace, nor as much of a punishment….."[97]

The tax laws, not achieving their purpose, were amended so that legal whiskey distilleries became economically attractive for the landowners and the small illicit stills unprofitable. This occurred in the mid 1820's and it was noted that by 1840 the area had grain to sell out of the district where before the whiskey makers had used so much there had sometimes been a shortage.

---

[96] Reminiscences of my life in the Highlands vol 2 Joseph Mitchell p 61
[97] ibid pg 311

Part 3

EARLY NINETEENTH CENTURY LIFE IN FORFARSHIRE SCOTLAND

Old Road, Glenesk

A family leaving the farm land of their forefathers but still farming in the Glens. Transport, sport, and gaun-aboot-bodies.......

The times of the parents of the emigrants John and Jane Storrier:

The Parents:
David Storrier married Janet McKenzie in 1809
Charles Duncan married Margaret Farquharson in 1831

Chapter 1

A Farming Family on the Move

The Storrier family had lived at Craigniety in the Parish of Glenisla for at least three generations when Janet, known as Jessie, McKenzie married David. On their wedding day in 1809 David was 33 and Elspeth 28. They, along with many other healthy highlanders were to have a large family. Even though they were not young when they married they still had eight children baptised in the following fifteen years. They would never have thought that a son of theirs, born to continue working on the land, was to finish his life in New Zealand. It is unlikely they had heard of New Zealand which had been put on the maps of the world first by Abel Tasman in 1642-3 and later by Captain Cook in his four voyages between 1769 and 1774. It was not until thirty years after the marriage of Janet and David that steps were taken to establish a British Colony in New Zealand.

It is not possible to know which of the ruined houses at Craigniety belonged to the Storriers. The ruins which still remain there today imply the design was on the "but and ben" format. These had the main living area, the but, at one end; at the other end was the ben which often had a wooden floor and a box bed for, the parents. The total floor space was 14 by 30 feet, there was a big stone fireplace on the eastern wall, a central doorway and two substantial windows[98] facing south each with four panes of glass thick enough to distort the view. These windows did not open, still, unless the weather was particularly inclement, the door was likely to have been left open. Should it have been shut and you had wanted to visit Jessie and David the custom was not to knock and wait, but to open the door and go on in, sure of a welcome as was the way in the Glens at this time. The peat fire inside was always smouldering and darkening the wooden beams in the ceiling.

This home in Craigniety was near or even the same dwelling that David (who was born in 1776) had grown up in. David's father was 62 when David and Janet married and David would have been taking over much of the farm work. In his father's time the Earl of Airlie's Factor had written strongly complaining about the ignorant practices in the farming methods at Craigneity and Sturt which did not get the best out of the soil. The tenants had bound themselves to new regulations which referred to liming of the fields, penning sheep to dung the fields, and stipulating what time of the year the sheep were to be taken to the hills. [99] Fertilizing the oat fields was hard work. The dung left by sheep penned over night in small stone and dirt yards had to be dug up and spread. Alternatively where there was lime it had to be dug as did the peat and both put in alternating layers inside a stone kiln to be

---

[98] Craigniety is an old location and the stone portals on doors and windows were of such a size that one wonders if they were the recycled parts of a more substantial building from the far past.

[99] This information from John Hardy, Lintrathen and Glenisla pg 5. This was in 1781 and the tenants concerned were Finlay Grewer living in Craigniety and his relative James Grewer was in Sturt; as tenants of the Earl of Airlie (whose enforced exile in France did not finish until 1783), these two had signed a document regarding the rental conditions at Craigniety and Sturt.

burnt then transferred to the fields.

How much this land had altered in the 40 years after this document is uncertain. But by the time John, Jessie and John Storrier's sixth child was born, the family had moved to Sturt, still within the Glenisla parish. There was no longer stability of families tenanting the same land generation after generation.

The Storrier family may have had to move because the land owner wanted an increase in rent which the Storriers could not afford. Someone who had the ability to fence, drain and fertilize the pastures could have profitably run more cattle. The Storriers may have lost access to invaluable common land where they had pastured sheep and obtained peat for essential fuel, although the Statistical Analysis notes that it was not until the twelve years following 1830 that "upwards of 10,000 acres of hill ground have ...been divided among those proprietors by whom they were formerly held in common". [100] It could be that this was when the grouse moors were developed for this was the era when the Highlands became popular for shooting and hunting. Wealthy Englishmen would pay well for a shooting holiday. The grouse butts where the shooters are positioned are marked on present day maps, and the cultivation of heather for the grouse made a profitable use of this land for the owners.

Sturt, meaning trouble and strife, does not sound inviting, and may not have been an improvement. If anything it was more isolated than Craigneity and Craighead which an 1820 map shows as having a clear track up to it from Glenisla whilst Sturt, situated on the Finlet Burn west of Craighead did not. Between Craigneity (310 metres above sea level) and Sturt

---

[100] p 434

(about 330 metres above sea level) was the Crock, a hill of 554 metres. Still in the parish of Glenisla it was not far from the farm of Glenmarkie, but in 1820 this did not have a well formed track in to it either. It was nearly two miles down to Glenisla, along Muckle Burn, then a mile or so beside the river Isla before heading up the Finlet Burn valley two miles to Sturt.

David Storrier and his wife Jessie with their five young children, the oldest being about ten and the youngest still breast fed, would have had to load their belongings on to the wicker baskets carried by highland ponies and trudge across rugged terrain to their new home. There were cousins around to help: Jessie's brother William at Craighead had married David's sister Jean a year after David and Jessie's marriage in 1809. Another of David's sisters, Elspeth was the wife of John Duncan at Craighead and they had ten children some of whom would still have been around to lend a hand.

They would have hoped for a fine day since all they would have had to cover their baskets would have been sheep skins and for themselves woollen shawls. A seventeen year old medical student had invented the process of making an India rubber waterproof cloth in 1816 but it is unlikely that the Storriers would have had access to this in 1820. It was not the young student whose name was to be remembered for this waterproof clothing but the Glasgow manufacturing chemist Charles McIntosh who developed and patented these garments.

The Storrier home at Craigneity was not abandoned; whoever held this land still required labourers but on a basis that the family could not provide. In 1841 the house is inhabited by four farm labourers and one girl, all with different names. The girl was 20 and registered as a farm servant, one wonders what her relationship was exactly with the houseful of young men and one older one. It was said that there was a shortage of farm workers' accommodation and that this led to "immorality and immigration." A Mr Corbett travelling Scotland at this   period was of the opinion that these unmarried farm workers who were not housed with the family lived in conditions worse than those of the horses or dogs on the farm.   There was often inadequate fuel and little to eat other than the agreed quota of oatmeal.

The Storrier family stayed at Sturt for the birth of two children, John in 1820 and his sister Susan two years later. Sometime later the family was on the move again, this time out of the parish of Glenisla[101] on to Brullion in the neighbouring parish of Lintrathen. Farm workers of this time frequently moved often with little pretext other than an altercation with the land lord. The dwellings they inhabited had no flower gardens or particular comforts inducing them to stay and since many were on the move it was possible to relocate.

At Brullion their last child Andrew was born. There they were not tenant farmers but employed as agricultural labourers and farm servants. As a family they would have got less cash in

---

[101] In 1829, after the Storriers had left, a "neat Free Church, with manse, was erected   chiefly at the expense of James Rattray of Kirkhillocks." It stood "at a little distance to the north of the Established Church. A school and schoolhouse, a small but comfortable hotel, and two or three cottages are in the immediate neighbourhood of the churches and manses, the whole forming a small hamlet called the Kirkton of Glenisla......a pleasant place for a summer retreat, but the little community must have a dreary, weary winter, cut off, as they sometimes are for weeks, from the busy world outwith the glen.." A J Warden p 349

wages than unmarried workers but would have the cottage rent free and in addition to the six and a half bolls or so of oatmeal would have kept a cow, hens and maybe a pig and some ground for growing vegetables and lint. In all David and Elspeth had eight children: Elizabeth, Margaret, Charles, Elspeth, William, John , Susan and Andrew.

Painting in Angus Folk Museum, Glamis

Chapter 2

Growing up in a Highland Glen [102]

Two years before John Storrier's parents, David and Janet, settled in to married life in Craigneity, Charles Duncan was born, a short walk up the hill at Craighead. Charles was 31 years older than David Storrier then living in neighbouring Craigneity, but it was his daughter Jane who was to marry John and go to New Zealand.

Charles was John and Elspeth Duncan's sixth child, with four more children coming in quick succession.. In winter young Charles walked over an hour down to the school at Glenisla Kirkton which he attended from age five or six until he was twelve or thirteen. Reading, writing and arithmetic were widely taught in Scotland. [103] No European country other than Prussia was said to have had such a comprehensive education system. The heritors (those who owned property) of each parish had to help support a school; parents had to pay a small amount per quarter per subject and learning was valued.

---

[102] The term Highlands was used for Glenisla and Lintrathen (see A J Warden, Angus or Forfarshire), although some may argue that they should be called Braes since Gaelic was not spoken.

[103] Northern and western Scotland, where little English and only Gaelic was spoken, did not have such an effective education system with many children kept home from school to work on the land even when schools were available.

Compared to England the education of the agricultural workers' children was encouraged. This is illustrated in a general survey in England requested by the government in 1808 from which Charles Vancouver produced a "General View of the Agriculture of the County of Devon". On the introduction of village Sunday Schools and Dame schools for the general populace which were "promoted by their present Majesties (George III and Queen Charlotte)" Mr Vancouver pronounced that "he looked forward with dread to the consequences of such a measure." After all, "if education would result in the labourer being more moral and more desirous of excelling in his work then it might be of public benefit." But he was certain the opposite effect was likely as, for example in Ireland, where teaching people to read had led to a "desire to ramble" and thus to emigration. It gave peasants ambitions that were entirely unsuitable for "those whose path in life is distinctly marked out". He believed the keenness of the Scottish folk to migrate stemmed from the education they received when young; any measure that makes people restless must prove harmful to the community.

It was therefore the surveyors opinion that every means should be made available to make labourers want to excel, whether at breaking stones for lime kilns or repairing highways. As a further warning on the dangers of allowing literacy to spread among the workers he begged the question, "how can mutinies and uprisings be avoided if the multitude can correspond with one another?"[104]

Fortunately for our Charles Duncan the sixteenth century work of John Knox had largely led to a very different attitude to education throughout Scotland where good citizenship was

---

[104] Devon Family History no 125 February 2008 from article by Brenda Powell. Pages 32-33.

thought to follow from a knowledge of the scriptures, which, in sound Protestant ethos it was felt should be read by everyone. Following the realisation in the eighteenth century that the Parochial schools had not accomplished this the Society for the Propagation of Christian Knowledge, the SPCK, was born. This organisation successfully set up schools throughout the highlands and there was one up river from Glenisla at Folda. However "Both schools just now (1790) are in bad repair, and truly it is difficult to get these matters properly adjusted among such a number of heritors, " wrote the Rev. Donald. Schools were well attended in the winter months but the children were needed on the land especially for herding during the summer.

The schools these boys attended, in winter time at least, until their early teens were often run by long standing and long suffering teachers. Teachers at this time were poorly recompensed, often less than that of a ploughman and only a fraction of what the minister in the parish was given. They were sometimes bright children whose parents had not been able to afford the cost of a full university education, or if they had managed to complete had not been able to secure a post as a minister. The manse was likely to be a much superior building to the teacher's or the school house. To take the example of the neighbouring parish of Lintrathen in 1790 where "the parochial schoolmaster has a salary of 6 or 7 bolls of oats, collected from the tenants, and some trifling fees. On this miserable allowance he has contrived to support a family upwards of sixty years. The hut in which he resides is hardly fit to accommodate the meanest beggar."[105]

John McKenzie, four years senior to Charles Duncan, remembered how the schoolmasters would augment their

---

[105]　Statistical Account Lintrathen number xxxv pg 566

pitiful salary on the annual school cockfighting day: "…it is a *fact*, and it was universally the custom in the Highlands. I remember that the fighting lasted from breakfast till the evening, the children of each family having to produce a fighting cock, unless they were *disgracefully* poor indeed. The teacher presided, and many of the parents attended to see fair play. The teachers' salaries were truly homeopathic and every cock killed in the school, and I think the fugies (runaways) also, were the teacher's perquisite. And as in a large school, the numbers of these was great, his salary was perceptibly helped by the dead cocks and the sale of the fugies. I have no recollection of the parochial laws on the subject. All I know is that I never heard of a clergyman finding fault with the barbarity, and that we young savages delighted in the devilry, as much as Spaniards enjoy bull-baiting in more civilised times."[106]

However long Charles stayed at school his success in farming and acquiring property later in life suggest that he would have been an able student. It is likely that he learnt well how to read, write and do arithmetic, and that from this he would have kept a careful log book of his income and expenditure.

Around 1818 when Charles was eleven years old he probably left home to work. His experience could have been similar to that of James Smith born in 1805 who later recalled -
"About the twelfth year of my age I was engaged to a farmer to herd his cattle the farm being about five miles to the west…..the engagement being for the summer six months. I do remember when I arrived I though I had landed in a foran land. Never before had I been a night out of my Father's house - for all the six months I did not expect to see them - however I

---

[106] Pigeon Holes of Memory p 96

liked the employ very well and I got strong always being in the fresh county air. I do remember well my mother came one Sunday to see me to ascertain how I was getting on - when I beheld my mother coming across the field you may fancy what a joy sprang up in my heart - what a blessed meeting it was to me and no doubt a joy and comfort to her part to find her little boy well and running amongst the grass - but ....she immediately put the question to me laddy says she do you get food enough this unexpected salutation threw me...and I for sometime could not answer the question. she held me to the point and of course I had to explain to her the sort of treatment I was receiving - she declared when she saw me there was something a wanting - I at this time of life being natural quiet and never being from home the advantage of me was taken by the old woman - as a mother she should have known better - at the meal time I was sat down well by myself and got a share of what was going it being put in to a little dish..........my mother saw by my appearance that really I was starved. From that time I had courage and when at meal time my dish were empty I asked for some more.

As the end of summer approached James "longed for the hour of departure...to enjoy again my Father's fireside , my Mother, sisters and brothers and not only that but I held in mind another joy which was before me that was my wages which I wrought hard for , it being the first ever earned." When the day did arrive he set off for home with confidence until he came to a mure [bog lands] "which I had to cross without any house in it. It was here when a thought ran through my mind. I have my money in my pocket and it may be I may meet a robber by the ways and rob me of all my six months earning. What should I do? I resolved and took the handkerchief from my neck and put the money in rolling it up and put it around my neck. Standing still for a little looking to the right and to the left to see if I should see any person I at the same time took my shoes and stockings held them in my hand and you may fancy I was not long in the mure ....I got clear of this and landed once more at my Father's fireside and as |I related my journey to my father and all they gave me great praise for my cunning craft."

After this James went back to school for the winter. Often boys would return to school if they did not have work and it was not uncommon to have odd "mature" students in the classroom. The following summer James was engaged by a farmer as herd boy : "I might mention here the Farmer was Factor for Col. Grant Cullin. He was not married. His mother lived with him on the farm as housekeeper his only sister along with him they were a very exemplary family a nice old lady very good to all her servants especially to the boy....stayed here four years - by this time getting too big for a herd boy so I left."[107]

These early forays from home were often to neighbours or relatives, but boys also went in to market days for the hiring of servants. On such a day in Fettercain the following anecdote is recorded to illustrate "the cool self-sufficiency of these young servants of the Scottish type": A boy was asked by a farmer if he wished to be engaged. "Ou ay," said the youth. Wha was your last maister?" was the next question. "Oh, yonder him," said the boy; and then agreeing to wait where he was standing with some other servants till the inquirer should return from examination of the boy's late employer. The farmer then returned and accosted the boy, "Wel, lathie, I've been speering' about ye, an' I'm tae take ye." "Ou ay," was the prompt reply, "an' I've been speerin' about ye tae, an' I'm nae gaen."[108]

---

[107] Memoirs of James Smith, Dundee City Archives (GD/Mus 29/1)
[108] Reminiscences of Scottish Life and Character, Dean Ramsay p254

The Kirk when Charles attended as a boy was possibly a more colourful place than it had been fifty years ago. At least the Highland church round 1812 which is described by Elizabeth Grant was - "....old grey-haired rough visaged men that had known my grandfather and great-grandfather, black, red, and fair hair, belonging to such as were in the prime of life, younger men, lads, boys - all in the tartan. The plaid as a wrap, the plaid as a drapery, with kilt to match on some, blue trews on others, blue jackets on all. The women were plaided too, an outside shawl was seen on one, though the wives wore a large handkerchief under the plaid, and looked picturesquely matronly in their very high white caps. A bonnet was not to be seen, no Highland girl ever covered her head; the girls wore their hair neatly braided in front, plaited up in Grecian fashion behind, and bound by the snood, a bit of velvet or ribbon placed rather low on the forehead and tied beneath the plait at the back. The wives were all in homespun, home-dyed linsey - Woolsey gowns, covered to the chin by the modest kerchief worn outside the gown. The girls who could afford it had a Sabbath day's gown of like manufacture and very ornamented with a string of beads, often amber; some had to be content with the best blue flannel petticoat and a clean white jacket, their ordinary and most becoming dress, and few of these had either shoes or stockings; but they all wore the plaid, and they folded it around them very gracefully.

"They had a custom in the spring of washing their beautiful hair with a decoction of the young buds of the birch trees. I do not know if it improved or hurt their hair, but it agreeably scented the Kirk, which at other times was wont to be over powered by the combined odours of snuff and peat reek, for the men snuffed immensely during the delivery of the English sermon; they fed their noses with quills fastened by strings to the lids of their mulls, spooning up the snuff in quantities and without waste. The old women snuffed too, and groaned a great deal, to express their mental sufferings, their grief for all the backslidings supposed to be thundered at from the pulpit; lapses from faith was their grand self-accusation, lapses from virtue were, alas! little commented on; temperance and chastity were not in the Highland code of morality..........."[109]

These well dressed women in Kirk did not necessarily come from well to do houses, as the Rev'd Donald M'Rae noted that folk of his parish in 1836 came from not "particularly clean" homes yet " when the young people go to Kirk or market, few appear more trig or clean; and a stranger would hardly be persuaded that some of them lived in such miserable hovels. When a girl dresses in her best attire, her very habiliments, in some instances, would be sufficient to purchase a better dwelling-house than that from which she has just issued."[110]

The sermon in Charles' time was still a dramatic affair. His contemporary John McKenzie recalls the preacher   the Rev. Kennedy of Killearan, being a great favourite. " One who was present at Communion where he was helping told me that, after the fencing of the tables to prevent the young and timid from communicating, when all were seated he suddenly shouted, "I see Satan seated on some of your backs," whereupon several screamed and more than one fainted and had to be removed. None of your milk and water preachers! The sensational is alone of use."[111]

A little further up from the church and the school was Gallows

---

[109] op cit Memoirs of a Highland Lady 1797-1827 (1897)

[110] Pigeon Holes of Memory p49

[111] A Hundred Years in the Highlands pg 158

Hill which Charles and his school friends would have known as the place where a gibbet had stood in the past. It had been "erected for those unfortunate persons, whom the servile court of a despotic baron had condemned to death" as the friend of the statistical account described the gallows hill in Lintrathen. He clearly considered that in 1790 he was living in a more democratic and sympathetic era. In Lintrathen the pile of stones below Gallows Hill were said to be the vestiges of the hangman's habitation. [112]

Transportation to Australia provided an alternative to hanging in the nineteenth century but there were still two hundred and forty men and women hanged. Public hanging continued until 1865 and while the trials might be moved elsewhere the hanging would be held nearer the place where the crime had been done. This created a major logistic problem for the city elders as hangings had become a rarity: Who would be hangman? How much would he be paid? Did he need an assistant? Did they need to pay his travel expenses ("he" in Forfarshire tended to come from Dundee or Edinburgh); Where should the gallows be placed? How were they to be constructed? And then what was to be done with the body….sometimes this was buried in the prison precincts but usually it was claimed by Edinburgh physicians for dissection. One doctor collected skulls as he had a theory that criminals had a particular skull shape.

These hangings were public as a major justification for them was the belief that the event would act as a deterrent. This is most clearly expressed in a pamphlet well circulated in 1847:

---

[112]   stat account 1791-99 vol 13 p563

IMPORTANT TO THE PUBLIC

An interesting and moral Exhibition of "KILLING ACCORDING TO LAW" will take place, in Dundee, on Wednesday Morning the 22d instant. To enlighten the people and terrify the Mob, one of our fellow-creatures will be hanged by the neck until dead.

Our Christian Government!!!! With a praiseworthy desire to illustrate and enforce the benevolent doctrines of Christ, will willingly allow all to behold the humanizing and gratifying Spectacle - Gratis!!!

As the sight - of a Hangman vindicating the "Sacred Majesty of the Law" --- is only intended for the vile, the vicious, and the depraved, it is sincerely to be hoped ,if there be even one decent woman, and one respectable man present, that they will STAND ASIDE and allow the degraded women and demoralised men to get as close to the Scaffold as possible.

In conclusion, all Mothers who are wicked, drunken and debased, and all Women destitute of modesty, virtue, and religion, are expected to be present. Be punctual to the hour.

Charles would certainly have known about the hangings in Montrose and Forfar in 1821 and 1826. Broadsheets were the equivalent of twentieth century tabloids, rapidly publishing lurid details of such crimes as they came to hand. Then on the day of execution folk would come in from the surrounding country side and swell the crowds to witness the event which with the tolling of church bells, the singing of hymns, the

133

accused's last speech to the crowd, the rolling of drums, let alone the contortions of the body when the person was finally dropped, combined to form an unforgettable spectacle. There was too the added tension at time of uncertainty as to whether the person had or had not committed the crime.

The Montrose execution was of Margaret Shuttleworth found guilty of battering her husband to death with the poker following "…..too much indulgence in spirituous liquor [that] had wrought you up to a species of frenzy, which in the end proved fatal to your deceased husband." Despite the rain coming down in torrents and the winds battering the seaside town there were over four thousand people crowded around the Market Cross to watch the event, along with the 360 special constables who had been brought in to keep law and order. And afterwards even in Session Books of Montrose it was reported as follows: "1821 December 7. MARGT. TINDAL was executed in front of the jail, for the supposed murder of her husband HENRY SHUTTLEWORTH, having been condemned upon presumptive proof."[113]

The Forfar hanging was of another woman, Margaret Wishart, for poisoning with arsenic her sister and her sister's child. The motive was seen as jealousy for the sister who was blind and who had become pregnant twice from one Andrew Roy who had come on the scene as Margaret's "intended".

Most of the hangings in the Angus area were for the murder of a spouse although in 1835 Mark Devlin was hung for the rape of a fourteen year old girl. In general early nineteenth century Highlands seems to be a peaceable place; in Lethnot[114] for

---

[113] They Did Wrong by Jessie Sword` p22
[114] stat account 1790 vol pg

example folk could sleep without bolting their doors. In Glenisla the general character of the people was said to be "humane....and as decent in their behaviour as their neighbours around them"; they only had to watch out during sheep shearing time when the parish was "much infested with vagrants from different parts of the country."[115]

After Charles had grown to be too old to be a herd boy he may have gone to the WhitSunday or Martinmas[116] fairs where farm workers found employment. There was at this time a constant change of workers, a tendency to "flit" after a years engagement. The austere accommodation - often single men bothys were little more than sheds with bunks and a peat fire to heat their staple food of oatmeal and water - was not conducive to settling down for a long period. Young men from farms would present at the WhitSunday or Martinmas fairs at the Mercat Crosses[117] in market towns such as Brechin, Kirriemuir

---

[115]   stat account vol 6 pg 396

[116]   Whitsunday was the time when, after Jesus had been crucified and had ascended to heaven, the apostles were gathered together and suddenly began to speak in foreign languages which they had never knowingly learnt. Everyone was amazed and it was said they had been filled with the holy Spirit. Accordingly, Pentecost, as it was called, was a time favoured for baptisms, when it was hoped the child would receive he holy spirit as well as admission into the church. Martinmas was called after a Roman bishop and hermit, Saint Martin of Tours. At this time Martinmas was celebrated around 11 November and WhitSunday round 15 May. In 1886 these dates were regulated to: the 28th of February, (Candlemas), 28 May (WhitSunday) 28 August(Lammas = loaf mass or bread feast being the day of first fruits of harvest especially wheat) and 28 November (Martinmas).These quarterly dates which began as religious festivals also equate to the times of the 2 solstices when the days are at their shortest or longest, and the 2 equinoxes when daylight and night hours are most equal. They were the times when leasehold payments , rents, servants tenures were made and paid, hence the need to regularise the dates into the legal system.

[117]   Mercat cross was the Scottish term for the often substantial market

or Alyth. The tenant farmers who needed farm hands would be there to look for agricultural labourers and when a deal was done drink would flow.

cross. Reasons given for the cross are that it was there to obtain God's blessing on the trading, and/or to remind sellers not to defraud , or to warn townsfolk not to barter so hardthat the traders would not return. Men from Glenisla could walk to towns such as Forfar, Coupar Angus, Fettercain, Inverary and Dundee as well Kirriemuir, Brechin and Alyth, all of these had market places.

Chapter 3

Coaches, Pedestrians, "Gaun-aboot-Bodies"

"When I was a lad and very little
The only steam came from a kettle"

Men like John McKenzie and Charles Duncan who were born
in the Highlands at the beginning of the nineteenth century saw
huge changes in their world. During their lifetime   steam
shipping lines developed as did the networks of railway lines
and toll roads. But as children foot and horse transport limited
the parameters of their world.

Should Charles, as a young man, have had occasion to leave
the Glens a way out was to follow the track down to Alyth then
on southward to Coupar Angus. Here the Couttie Bridge (built
in 1766) crossed the River Isla and the Defiance Coach could
be picked up on its daily run from Edinburgh through Perth to
Aberdeen. If he had arrived early he may have stayed in the
hostelry at the White House (or Horse) Inn which was opposite
the Defiance Inn where the coach stopped. This stage coach
run had been set up by Captain Barclay in the late 1820's. In
the 1830's it was taken over by a group of country gentlemen
and prided itself on being punctual to the minute. Described as
having for its fifteen passengers "coaches luxurious and
hansom...drivers and guards in their uniforms of red coats and
yellow collars...the horses beautifully matched and of the first

character, harness in good taste....drivers were respectable men, steady, great favourites on the road, obliging, full of conversation and local knowledge. Several played with no mean talent on the bugle and cornet."[118] With its crack, scarlet liveried coachmen and wonderfully matched horses, it would leave Edinburgh at five and, despite the time taken crossing the Firth of Forth 10 miles from Edinburgh by Queen's ferry, would arrive in Perth forty miles on at nine o'clock.

John McKenzie described his journey on it -
"It was late ere I reached the coach office and found the coach full outside and in - except the box set which was, greatly to my surprise, at my service, and where I gladly seated myself. Had I known the pace, I'm not sure ... that I'd have been so glad of my good luck - with Ramsay of Barnton (an owner and frequent driver) as my whip. But I was in for it and innocent , till we had galloped (for trotting was impossible in the four hours time allowed) a mile or two, and then I had just to hold hard as the coach swung along like a pendulum, two wheels on the ground at once being plenty when going round a corner. However, we got safe to Glenfarg, where the road for a mile or two runs alongside a deep burn, winding so often and so much that only a few hundred yards are in sight at once. And it is only wide enough for sober folks and not made for racing four-in-hand coaches. We had wheeled round a corner and there , within a hundred yards, was a cart, its driver lying on his back without a rein or whip in hand. I took a look at Ramsay gathering up his reins and standing up, white enough in the cheek, the cart trailing along in the centre of the road, our guard's bugle awakening the dozing driver. I doubt if it took a minute ere our racers were up to and passing him like lightning, actually an inch or so from his wheels. He had sat

---

[118] Journey down the Ages Rev WD Chishom, 1983

up, and Ramsay being a master of the whip. I doubt if any mortal ever go such a thorough cutting-up of his chops by a whip lash s we scampered along. He just yelled with pain or fury, and looking back we saw him roll out of his cart n the road, fly to a heap of road metal, fill both hands and shower it after us - by that time a hundred yards away. For sound, and action, I don't remember ever observing a human being seem so crazed by passion . It was grand. Ramsay merely drew a long, relieved-like hissing breath, and raced away, not saying a word for a good while. I came then to understand why there were no passengers wanting the box seat till I cast up; in a smash there would be no one to act as a buffer ere reaching the horses heels!"[119]

For anyone going on to London from Edinburgh there was the Fifty-Six Hour Coach which never stopped "except to feed". The horses and coachmen were changed twenty-eight times between Edinburgh and London, so using one hundred and twelve horses each journey.[120] There was an alternative method

---

[119] Pigeon Holes of Memory p120-1, 131

[120] This was the height of horse and carriage transport. In 1822 when John McKenzie was a medical student aged 18 he went to London. One of his adventures was a day at Epsom races …"we two drove off in an open carriage , behind two spanking greys and a scarlet-coated postillion, in a charming summer day. And if what met me that day did not open a country bumpkin's eyes, it's a pity. How could anyone not bred yearly to the Derby have an imagination of that day's drive to Epsom, of the race ground, and more than all of the astounding drive home, after the regular battle to get from the race ground, upon the jammed-with-carriages road to town, …..half of London were crushed upon that road from daylight till dark; for now the horrid rail carries the mob who then drove, or rode, and very often finished by a walk to town, heaps of the carriages being in smithereens, from drivers having had too much dinner…..And all along the road were such crowds of people looking on at the battle and helping to drag the smashed-up carriages off the road." Pigeon Holes of Memory p 133-4

of going by sea but this before the days of steam was not always punctual as McKenzie found when it took him seventeen days to get from London to Findhorn having had to shelter from strong North winds for several days at Harwich and eight days at Yarmouth Roads. He then finished his journey home on foot.

Walking distances was commonplace. The founder of the Scottish Defiance coach run, Robert Barclay Allardice, had become famous for his walking prowess and was known as the "Celebrated Pedestrian". This title he earned from his exploits in long distance walking which was a popular sport in the eighteenth and nineteenth centuries. Huge crowds would gather to watch "Pedestrianism" , even paying at times for the sight. Wagers were taken on the outcome, the competitors themselves involved and able to win big money from this gambling side of the sport.

One of Barclay's most famous walks was in 1809 when he walked one mile in each of 1,000 successive hours, i.e. he walked a mile an hour every hour for 42 days and nights. Another pedestrian athlete Lieutenant Fairman wagered he could walk 60 miles in 14 hours. These walkers had trainers and assistants, training schedules and diets. Most shunned fish and vegetables as being insufficiently nutritious and water was taboo as unhealthy. The main fare was usually meat and beer. Barclay insisted on old, home brewed bottled ale. Fairman favoured bread soaked in Madeira. The pedestrians came in all sizes and shapes although it was generally thought that good wind and good bottoms (powerful gluteal muscles) were key attributes.

Captain Barclay as he was known due to his participation in the Napoleonic Wars was also a boxer and an accomplished stagecoach driver himself. It was said that he once drove the London mail coach single-handed from London to Aberdeen which entailed a non stop drive of nearly three days and nights. It was a horse that caused his death when he was 77 in 1854, as he died a few days after being kicked.

The mail coaches brought newspapers from the big cities and the exploits Barclay and such men would have been known to the likes of Charles even if the papers were not very hot off the press by the time he got to read them.

Charles grew up in an era when the roads were greatly improved. In the first twenty years of the century 920 miles of road and 1,117 bridges were built in the Highlands, so the wheeled vehicle was penetrating previously remote areas. "Those who were born to railroads, or even to modern mail-coaches, can scarcely be made to understand how we, of the previous age, got on, The state of the roads may be judged from two or three facts, There was no bridge over the Tay at Dunkeld or over the Spey at Fochabers, or over the Findhorn at Forres, nothing but wretched, peer-less ferries, let to poor cottars, who rowed, or hauled, or pushed a crazy boat across, or more commonly got their wives to do it."[121] So wrote Lord Cockburn (28 years senior to Charles) describing the state of the roads at the turn of the century.

Charles Duncan may or may not have ventured far along these roads. Yet they impacted upon life in the glens, the farming finally departing from the traditional communal ways. From being the son of a farmer who had a small holding Charles became the farm manager of large tracts of land and the owner of several properties. Other boys from similar backgrounds

---

[121] Pigeon Holes of Memory p 65

would have left the land and gone to live in a town, or remained as farm labourers frequently moving and not having their own plot to work or their own animals to rear.

At some point Charles moved to Lintrathen and obtained the tenancy of McRitch midway up the Backwater valley above the Lintrathen Loch. He was likely a strong young man with a straight back and a powerful torso and an energetic and optimistic turn of mind. By the time he was twenty four he had won the hand in marriage of Margaret Farquharson, the only child of Robert and Jean Farquharson. Robert and Jean Farquharson were farmers a mile or more up the Backwater valley from McRitch. Margaret's mother Jean had been Jean Low before she was married and it was possibly through her that Charles and Margaret came to live at McRitch as McRitch had been tenanted for many years by the Low family. It was part of the Airlie Estate and as such Charles would have been the tenant of John Ogilvy.

Charles and Margaret's family grew quickly: in 1832 and 1833 sons were born and in 1835 and 1837 two daughters. These children were named in the traditional Scottish way. The first born male taking the name of the fathers father, in this case John; the second born son the name of the mother's father, this being Robert. The first girl took the name of her mother's mother, Jean. And the second girl was named after her mother, Margaret. It is this repetition of names which can confuse later generations and leads to many holding the same name.

Margaret's parents, Robert and Jean (known also as Jane) Farquharson lived not far up the Backwater valley at Corriffie. After the birth of young Jean Duncan Grandfather Robert Farquharson died. His wife Jean/Jane continued to live and farm at Corriffie until her death in 1853 aged 85 and being the mother of Margaret was likely to have had a close relationship with the growing family.

Farquharson Clan [122]

Another baby girl, Ann, was born in 1841. This was the year the census of the Scottish people (or Scotch people as Queen Victoria called them) was taken. Nine folk were living in the McRich home which at this time had just three windows. In one ground floor room with the fireplace at one end was the cooking and living area . On the other side of the front door was the bedroom of Charles and Margaret with young Ann. Upstairs in loft rooms with little head room or light two rooms:

---

[122] By marrying Margaret Farquharson the New Zealand descendents have a gateway ancestor through whom they can trace lineage back to the fifteenth century to Finla Mor Farquharson, see Jean Hay "A Highland Heritage"

one for the males including the two sons John and Robert (although Robert aged 10 was not home on the night the census man came) and two farm workers, George Davidson who was 22 and 15 year old Andrew Storrier. The other room for the girls, Jean the oldest being 6, sharing a bed with her younger sister 3 year old Margaret, and perhaps another bed for the two farm servants who also lived in, 13 year old Margaret Dunn and 15 year old Jean Fraser. It was a full household and remained so for the next twenty years.

Also at McRitch were two other occupied dwellings, one housing Alexander Coulls, an agricultural labourer, and his wife and two children. The other smaller dwelling housed Charles' 64 year old mother Elspeth and his sister Ann, unmarried at 40. Visiting Scotland for the first time in 1842 and in the neighbouring shire Queen Victoria noted in her diary how "The country and the people have quite a different character from England and the English. The old women wear close caps, and all the children and girls are barefooted. I saw several handsome girls and children with long hair; indeed all the poor girls from sixteen and seventeen down to two or three years old, have loose flowing hair; a great deal of it red." Although if the New Zealand Duncan descendants are a guide it would seem this household had fine fair to dark brown but not red hair. Prince Albert commented that "many of the people look like Germans. The old women with that kind of cap which they call a "mutch", and the young girls and children with flowing hair, and many of them pretty, are very picturesque; you hardly see any women with bonnets."[123]

After John, Robert, Jean, Margaret and Ann came the births of

[123] Queen Victoria's Highland Journals edited by David Duff London 1980 p19-20

James (1842), Catherine (1844), Charles (1847) and Janet (1852). All nine children survived their childhood but in 1846 just when he would have left home to work on another farm the oldest boy John died. In 1851 it was still a very full and young household with seven family members and a 14 year old farm servant, a 25 year old shepherd and a 20 year old domestic servant; plus, on census night a visitor , a 23 year old agricultural labourer. The occupants of the Coulls' house have changed to the Dickonson family while William McDougall and his daughter occupy a smaller one. There is an uninhabited dwelling and Elspeth and Ann Duncan have disappeared from the scene. Charles was described as being a farmer of 60 acres and employing three men and two boys. All in all a large household to be head of.

It was during this time that Charles began to acquire his own property. In January 1847 it is recorded that Charles Duncan, residing at McRitch "...seized in the southwest and north most halves of a piece of land in the Northmuir of Kirriemuir...[and] two acres of Kirkton Infield land and another piece or portion of Muir ground between the aforesaid portion and the Road from Meikle Mill to Cortachy..."[124] He was to go on to own houses with rooms and offices to let in Tillyloss and Northmuir at Kirriemuir as well as being the tenant farmer at McRitch.

In 1851 Margaret at 44 years had her hands full. Pregnant with her last child Janet, she just had 20 year old Margery Alexander to help with the household chores. Fifteen year old Jean and 13 year old Margaret had left, probably to work in another household as domestic servants. There were Ann 10

---

[124] Sasines 519 16/1/1847. PR 300 282 and Sasines 520 16/1/1847 PR 300 284

years, James 8, Catherine 6, all of whom went to school, Charles 3 to be cared for. Then there was son Robert 17 and the

Northmuir, Kirriemuir.

Photo: Angus Council, Cultural Services

14 year old farm servant David Malcomnd and Thenthe 25 year old shepherd John Bryson plus their guest Alexander Forsyth living in the house. That is eleven people to cook and clean for. It is also eleven people to share the work load for both domestic and farm work was very labour intensive. All save young Charles would have their duties.

On wash days a deep, oval, tin bath painted yellowish brown on the outside and cream inside would be brought out and filled by buckets with water. It had a moulded handle at each end for lifting. A ridged wooden board and long bars of yellow soap to scrub the grubbier parts. After rinsing it was spread outside on the bleaching green; it was felt that a good frost was good for the washing and certainly it made the linen sparkle. Once dried children helped to stretch and fold the sheets and table cloths, pulling them evenly into shape. Finally a heavy, solid flat iron heated on the fire was used to press the garments and household linen.

Soap was one of the items which could be bought from one of the "gaun-aboot-bodies" or itinerant salesmen such as those described by Amy Stewart: "Charlie Timmer...was a regular caller...in summer he called every week peddling bootlaces and matches, acquiring pokes of tea and sugar, and his tinny filled with freshly made tea. He did odd jobs on farms, sleeping in shed or barn." Then there was "Besom Jamie who came round regularly with besoms(brooms) for sale, and slept in hospitable barns. To see him at his work it looked easy, but it was not a case of taking a bunch of birch twigs, tying them with string and putting a stick thought the middle. He made birch brooms for outdoor use in the garden or round the steading, and there was a real knack in the way he tied his bundles of twigs together. He made besoms and pot-rinsers from heather, with birch wood handles. The besoms were excellent for stone floors and were very durable. ....Besom Jamie died, full of years, in the Aberdeen "Poor's Hoose" and Charlie Timmer died of exposure on the Donside hills."[125]

Then there were tinkers who lived in tents. They did some poaching and made and sold spoons, pegs, and baskets from willow and pliable rowan or hazel for the rims. The women would be seen tramping the Glen at a steady pace, at least one of them carrying a baby tucked into her shawl. Yet another caller who Amy recalled was Mackie the Pig Man. He was quite well-to-do and had a pony and cart to carry his crockery which was called "pig" hence his name.

---

[125] Hills of Home by Amy Stewart Fraser p 175. Amy grew up in the Grampians near Ballater, north east of Lintrathen.

147

During these busy years Charles Duncan had not lost contact with the Storrier family he had known as a boy in Glenisla. Back in 1841 he had engaged their youngest son Andrew as a worker on McRitch . The Storrier family now living at Brullion in Lintrathen had another son John. He was older than Andrew and in fact fifteen years older than Jean Duncan. Yet it was John who courted and wanted to marry Charles' oldest daughter Jean, known as Jane.

Perhaps when Jane came home to be married the photograph which was to end up in New Zealand was taken. It was of Jane and her mother Margaret. Her mother is seated, somewhat slumped with the tiredness caused by childbearing and illness already showing. Her daughter is standing, straight and strong. Both are well attired in warm long full skirted dresses, waisted, with long sleeves and high necks. They have not adopted the impractical London fashion of enormous hooped crinoline skirts. Their long hair is parted in the middle and drawn back and up behind their heads. Another photo, probably taken at the same time as it is in the same Victorian dress, shows Jean standing alone on a carpeted floor; proud of her literacy, she is holding a book and has her hands lightly resting on a chair[126], behind her are long curtain drapes covering a large window. This photo was likely taken in a studio perhaps in the growing town of Kirriemuir where Charles was to buy some property of his own.

---

[126] the chair looks like one cabinet makers referred to as Victorian balloon backed and was made in a wood such as mahogany, rosewood or walnut, made by a skilled cabinet maker.

Photo: author's family album

This would have been a happy time, preparing the trousseau of blankets, perhaps tapestry or patch work bedspread, pillow and bolster cases, towels, tablecloths and sheets. And for herself the undergarments: cotton chemises, cotton drawers which tied around the waist, long cotton nightdresses and for winter flannel chemises, nightgowns and petticoats and aprons. Probably too some corsets with stiffly boned stays and fastened at the back with laces which were pulled tight to give the tiny waistline.

Growing up in Lintrathen in the same era as Jane was Mary Crighton[127] who was later to publish her book of poems and amongst them was one describing the loch in their parish:

---

[127] Poems by Marty Crighton published Dundee 1872

The Loch of Lintrathen

Encirled by Lord Airlie's lands
Lintrathen Loch securely stands
Where crag and wood form beauty wild,
Romantic spot for Nature's child.

Whoe'er has walked thy border round
Nor stopped to mark its shady bound
A cool retreat in summer day
From busy world and scorching ray.

How beautiful in summer time
When all is peaceful and sublime,
When woodland-music charms the ear,
To view they waters calm and clear!

To cheer the breeze with sweet perfume,
Around thee bright the wild flowers bloom;
With beauty Art can ne'er outvie,
Tho' she should paint in rarest dye.

Each varying form and varying hue
Proclaims aloud that praise is due
To Him who keeps, and who has formed
As hand of man hath ne'er adorned.

Thus summer robed, and softly smiled,
Is beauty lost in winter wild;
It cannot be: 'tis printed there,
'Twill but a sterner aspect wear.

Mary's poems echoing Sir Walter Scot's admiration for the Scottish landscape wrought by the Creator suggests how Jane may have viewed the land where she grew up.

An artist's romantic view of farming in Scotland

Part 4
MID NINETEENTH CENTURY LIFE IN FORFARSHIRE SCOTLAND

Carmylie farm workers with an experimental harvester. Photo: *Angus Council, Cultural Services*

Marriage in Lintrathen, death among the old and the young, move to Carmylie, education for the young, town life in Forfar, the departure for the New World, travel, sailing ship life and arrival in New Zealand.

The times of the Emigrants, John and Jane Storrier

John married Jane Storrier in 1854
Their children: Margaret b 1855, Elizabeth b. 1857, John 1859, Charles b. 1860, James b. 1862, David b. 1870.

Chapter 1

Victorian Scotland – marriages, births and deaths

John Storrier and Jane Duncan[128] were married at McRitch, the Lintrathen farm house where Jane grew up. In Scotland marriages could take place anywhere so long as there was a recognised minister and two witnesses present. And, unlike England minors under 21 could marry without their parents approval. [129] Not that there is any reason to think that the parents of John and Jane did not approve of this marriage, although John was fifteen years older than Jane; John was 34 and Jane 19 years old. Indeed finding a partner for marriage could not have been so easy as the Lintrathen community was still a small relatively static one.

Their wedding was a mid summer one, in August of 1854. There would not have been wedding invitations, the bride and bridegroom inviting folk by word of mouth. The

---

[128] Christened Jean she was known as Jane in New Zealand and will be referred to as Jane from now on.

[129] The ability for young people to marry without parental consent was why elopers would head north from England to Gretna Green. In 1856 a Scottish law stated that the couple had to be resident in Scotland for 21 days before they could marry and this was not repealed until 1977. Thousands of weddings are performed at this southern Scottish border village each year.

*Gretna Green, the blacksmiths famous forge where many marriages have taken place over the years photo: Angus Council, Cultural Services*wedding presents were of "eatables and drinkables" and included much whiskey from home stills. And perhaps if the heather was blooming early that year some ale made from its flowers, for with yeast and sugar added it was ready for use in a few days. Old customs still prevailed with partying beginning the Saturday before the proclamation of the banns. The night before the marriage there was the traditional "washing" of the bridegroom's feet with soot from the chimney. The Storrier and Duncan marriage was recorded in the Lintrathen Old Parish Register:

"John Storrier and Jane Duncan , both in the Parish, were regularly proclaimed for Marriage, and no objection offered to prevent them from being united."

On the day of the wedding of his eldest daughter Charles Duncan no doubt had many pipers and fiddlers there, much dancing and firing of guns and pistols to mark the event.

A romanticised portrayal of a highland wedding

The year of Jane's marriage her mother, Margaret, became weak and had a bad cough. For two years she struggled on, dying in the cold January weather of 1856 at five in the afternoon in her bed at McRitch. She was 49. She had been attended to by the surgeon James Mair from Alyth. The cause of death is recorded as phthis of the lungs, the Greek word for consumption and one commonly used then. It is possible that Margaret and Charles' three teenage children who died (John, the oldest boy, when he was just 14, Catherine at 15 and Janet at 16) also had consumption. Tuberculosis or TB as it is now commonly called was the most common cause of death among young adults.

Fevers, sore throats and coughs were common and it was not known then how the fatal disease of consumption was caught. It was also called vampire disease since those with it became very pale and weak. There was the idea that it was caused by "corruption of the air" and it was widely held to be important to have rooms well ventilated.[130] It was also common for those near the end to become optimistic, a light headed happiness.

Margaret's funeral was a sombre occasion. Robert as the eldest son and his father had formally called on every house around to deliver invitations. On the day the minister came to hold a short service around the black coffin inside the house, the weather being so cold. Present were Charles, his oldest son Robert then 23, Jane and John with their two month old child and the other children of Charles and Margaret: Margaret 18, Ann 15, James 13, Catherine 11, Charles 8 and young Janet, 3 years old. Every man from the Backwater valley who was able was there as a matter of courtesy. After, the coffin was taken miles down the road to the hallowed church yard of Glenisla for burial. The women stayed at home leaving the funeral procession and ceremony at the graveside to the men.

In winter with the ground covered in icy or sludgy snow even a horse and sleigh could have problems so the younger men took it in turns to carry the coffin; at intervals an older man would call out 'ither fower' and four fresh men would step forward to relieve the tired bearers. There was dignity and solemnity in the procession and any stranger meeting it removed his hat and stood aside respectfully. That same week Charles and his family would also have attended the funeral of Charles' oldest sister Janet who had died two days before Margaret. Unlike her relatively well to do sister in law she did not have a doctor in attendance and the cause of death is not known. Nor was Janet carried to Glenisla, but was buried in

---

[130] "Foul" air was thought to cause tuberculosis until after 1882 when Koch, developing the work of Louis Pasteur who had identified microscopic living organisms, came up with the "germ" theory.

the Lintrathen church yard, her husband William Thomas being present.

Charles continued to farm at McRitch for the next twenty or so years. The house remained a lively one full of children and grandchildren, typical of Victorian households with a mixture of generations of related folk and unrelated domestic and farm help. There was a lot of work to be shared out in these larger farm homes with their furnishings and "modern" trappings. Everyone worked, it was not an "upstairs downstairs" household where all menial chores were done by servants. The year after Charles' wife died his nineteen year old daughter Margaret gave birth to Ann. Margaret did not marry Ann's father, a local lad by the name of Robertson, and continued to living at McRitch with her father[131] in the capacity of housekeeper.

Illegitimacy rates at this time were higher in Scotland than in England, and indeed, for most of Europe. The frequency and the acceptance of natural births varied within Scotland from area to area but was higher in rural than urban areas. Acceptance of the situation was illustrated by a Free Church Minister who quoted a woman as saying: "It was not so bad as if she had taken two pence that was not her own". The Minister commented "That woman was a fair type of the average church member in this district, neither better nor

---

[131] Eight years later Margaret gives birth to another girl, Agnes, whose father was William Smart . William, like Margaret, had grown up on a farm in Lintrathen but at this time he was working as a railway porter in Forfar. The following year Margaret and William married and they have another daughter Jane. Margaret's misfortune was that William suffered from an internal hemorrhage for seven days then died. This was in 1870 so Margaret returned to McRitch to be housekeeper again this time with her three girls.

worse." [132] One down to earth Scotsman's explanation was "Our sexual immorality and the high rate of illegitimacy, we explain thus. No thrifty man would buy a barren beast. Therefore, as we cannot buy our wives and sell them if they prove unprofitable, 'tis well to try them in advance." [133]

In any event where there was year round employment for girls in the house or on the farm. (Margaret was a farm labourer on McRitch when she had this first child). She had the ability to provide for this new arrival and previous lack of chastity was not seen as a bar to marriage. Indeed in Lanarkshire a minister recorded that most of his brides brought a string of children with them to the alter. Lanarkshire was an area where the hind system prevailed where a job would be advertised for a hind and half hind - an agricultural labourer and his woman, preferably with children. Some unmarried young men would have to find a woman to come with them if they wanted the job. Moreover, in Scotland, unlike England, if the parents of an illegitimate child married that child automatically became legitimate.

Had Margaret been a domestic servant in a big house without the means to keep her child the situation would have been very different as then she and the child might have been dependent on the charity of the local Parish and or workhouse. Since the Poor Laws of 1845 the state had begun to take more responsibility for the very poor but living on charity was still shunned and seldom gave adequate provision. And should a woman have no alternative but to enter a dreaded workhouse she would forfeit the right to be responsible for her own child.

---

[132] Attributed to Cunninghame Graham, 18th century politician.
[133] Ibid p168

Chapter 2

Changing Parishes in Search of work: Carmylie

While Margaret continued to live at McRitch, John and Jane moved to Carmylie. Carmylie was a nearby parish lying south east of Lintrathen. There John was a tenant farmer on a farm called Westhills. He hoped to prosper here and to give his wife and family the life his father in law had made for himself. It was a small parish and the Reverend Patrick Betch who wrote the 1791-99 statistical account was not impressed. "...Carmylie furnishes very little scope for statistical inquiry.... about 3 miles long from east to west, and about 4 miles broad. It may be called a hilly and mountainous tract of ground...The land is wet and spongy and was thought ... ..to be better adapted for pasture than for grain." Nevertheless in the late nineteenth and early twentieth century the three landowners of this Parish had supported farm improvements. Much boggy ground was drained and fertilised and in places fenced; and there were significant increases in the yields from arable farming.

The farm the Storriers tenanted was of eighty acres. Their neighbours, the Alexander family, farmed the same acreage. The other families in the area were crofters with between eight and twenty acres, a few linen weavers and several stone quarriers. Throughout the nineteenth century great quantities of red and grey sandstone were taken from upland Carmylie; slates for roofs, stones for building and many slabs for pavements were quarried and sent to the nearest seaport,

160

Arbroath. From here it was exported, much finding its way to the footpaths still being trodden today in Glasgow and London. By the time the Storriers arrived many of the quarries were deep under ground and water had to be pumped out, so the landscape included moveable wooden windmills for this work.. An advantage of all the quarrying was the availability of reject stones which helped improve the standard of the workers homes.

The farm house which John and Jane moved in to was probably substantially built with a sound slate roof. Heated by coal which was brought back to Carmylie on the stone merchants return journey, it was dry and relatively warm. Pride of place in the kitchen would be the dresser with cupboards and drawers and china plates on the racks above. The wooden seats and scrubbed wooden table there for the family meal which would begin with prayers. This was not a household where the dinner time habits had disappeared with the kail-brose as a Minister of the church had predicted would happen: "The social and substantial dish, and especial favourite of our forefathers "the kail-brose of auld Scotland" is now in a great measure unknown among the younger generation; and very probably the brose-bicker disappeared with the gudeman from the table head, when, in the progress of refinement, he ceased to preside at the family board, around which the whole household used to assemble at meals, and where his presence and conversation produced the most beneficial effects on the manners and morals of the domestics."[134]

It was not to be a happy year for soon after moving, and within a year of her mother's death, John and Jane's first child died. Little Margaret was only two years old. There is no record of

---

[134] 1845 statistical account p 362

what caused her death.

Common causes of death for young children were communicable infections such as measles, chin cough (alias whooping cough), scarlet fever or consumption; or it was attributed to such problems as teething, bowel complaint, water in the head, nervous disease, worm fever or simply explained as decline. Death from teething remains something of a mystery although it is thought that since it occurred at the time many children were weaned it could have been contaminated milk; or again there was a practice of lancing the gums when they were inflamed and since conditions were not antiseptic this could have caused death from infection. The symptoms evident when a child was said to have died from teething were fretfulness, painful and swollen gums, convulsions and diarrhoea. There were too deaths from typhus fever spread by lice and fleas....it is difficult in this present century to control the spread of lice among young children so it cannot have been easy in those crowded nineteenth century dwellings.

Jane was already pregnant with her second child and in January 1857 Elizabeth was born at Carmylie. She was followed two years later by John and sixteen months later by Charles. By this time there were nine living in the house which was not large having just two windows. In addition to the family were Andrew Dick, an elderly agricultural labourer of 76 years, David Duncan and Andrew Norrie 18 and 16 respectively both ploughmen and Ann Craig, 20, a domestic servant.

John and Janet farmed at Carmylie for about twelve years[135]. After Margaret they had five more children, all born here at

---

[135] The valuation roll for 1867/8 has John Storrier as the tenant of the west half of Westhills valued at £70pa

Westhills. Their first school was in Carmylie and the Soutar family who lived nearby had children of similar ages. Mr Soutar was a ploughman, in charge of a pair of fine horses, a pair of which did the work a team of six or eight oxen would have done the previous century. These horses had some Clysdale blood in them, making them bigger, stronger and more feisty than the old Highland horses. With hairy white feet and often of a red roan colour they were hansom additions to the countryside. The boys of these two families, the Storriers and the Soutars, may have been referred to

Carmylie School. Photo: Angus Council, Cultural Services

casually as "loons" and the girls as "queyns". There were age old versions of games to be played with hoops, kites, marbles and bools of baked clay; then there were skipping ropes, bows and arrows and catapults, each game having its season of popularity. The Storrier children must have had some good memories of this time because years later when two of the boys were settled in Timaru in far off New Zealand the home was named Carmylie.

As the full household of the Storrier family illustrated there was still a great deal of man power involved in farming. The threshing machine may have superseded the flail but it still took many men to bring in the harvest. "We would... watch the team at work. One forked up a sheaf, another cut the band with a sharp knife and fed the sheaf into the body of the mill. Down the chute rushed the golden straw and a third worker immediately forked it away to be built into a sugar-loaf stack. Meantime, we heard the grain come hissing down with a dry rattle and a swishing sound into the sack held ready to receive it.....At the other side of the threshing machine the chaff scattered and made the workers cough as the scaly husks flew about, but though the steady drone ....they laughed and shouted happily to each other." [136] The machinery had an interest for the young Storrier boys who were later to enter the business of engineering, manufacturing farm machinery.

Their interest could have been triggered by the parish minister of Carmylie at this time. The Reverend Patrick Bell was especially keen on engineering and before he was ordained he had invented the first reaping machine. He had pondered since boyhood on the ancient and onerous task of cutting the corn bent over double swinging a scythe and had successfully produced one of the first pieces of agricultural machinery in 1828. Bell did not take a patent out on his invention believing it should be accessible to everyone. Unfortunately this not only meant he never made any money, it also led to poor copies being made which put people off and delayed the expansion of his masterpiece.

Yet the farming in this area was no longer flourishing. After the initial flush when the land was improved the soil proved to be poor and the weather harsh. "In some instances, cultivation

---

[136] Hills of Home pp112/3

has been extended too far in reclaiming soils of very inferior quality, which, though they gave a tolerable return when the prices of grain were high, and upon the first application of lime or marl, now show a strong tendency to revert to their original

BELL'S REAPING MACHINE.

state of whins or broom, - which would be far more agreeable to the eye than the bleak appearance which they now exhibit, and might be more profitable than the miserable crops or scanty herbage which they now produce.

"Considering the high and exposed situation of the parish, plantations of wood are much wanted, both for ornament and shelter …the greater part of the parish has no protection from the north or east winds…."[137] Carmylie's "high and exposed situation" and the "cold and retentive subsoil" are blamed for the lateness of any sowing and planting; growth did not make much progress until near the end of June which in turn made for a precarious harvest with time available before the onset of colder times being so short.

Whatever the cause John and Jane decided to leave the district. The usual procedure for a departing tenant was for him to

---

[137] Statistical Analysis Carmylie, County of Forfar (1834-45) p377

organise a "roup" (a sale). There was no need for a list of goods to be given out as those coming would know all the stock and farm equipment. All the locals would be there and everyone was provided with home made ale by the seller. A person expected to buy plenty might be given honey ale made with honey and yeast, whilst others might have heather ale or treacle ale prepared in gallon pigs and served out from zinc pails into mugs -[138]

> "The unctioneer cam' doon wi' verra sma' persuasion
> Tae be in chairge o' the Occasion"

Bidding could become fast and reckless and it was not unknown for folk to return home the owner of equipment for which they had no use for. The departure from Carmylie marked the end of John's farming career in Scotland. The family's next home was in the town of Forfar at 114 East High Street.

Some Carmylie workman who provided examples of work off the farm and who may have influenced the young Storrier boys who became farm implement manufacturers in New Zealand..
Photo: Angus Council, Cultural Services

---

[138] The Hills of Home p201

Chapter 3

Move to Urban Life - Forfar

Entering Forfar from the south, nineteenth century
Photo : Angus Council, Cultural Services

Some time between 1864 and 1870 the Storrier family moved from the farm at Carmylie to the nearby town of Forfar. Forfar had changed radically since the early 18th century when it had been described as "a poor ill built small town of farmers, innkeepers and linen manufacturers."[139] The textile industry meant that by the mid 19th century it was said that "....Forfar has marched with the times, and is today one of the most

---

[139] The Royal Burgh of Forfar, Alan Reid, p 237

progressive of Scots provincial towns" and had " a suburban fringe [which] has added grace to the grey old capital".[140] John and Jane were one family of hundreds which came to live in Forfar during this time. The population grew from 7,969 in 1841 to 12,057 in 1891. The census during these years showed how many residents had come from outside Forfar to live in this town where there was "great pride in the progress and place of Forfar."

The Storriers took up residence in the centre of town at 114 East High Street. This was a respectable if not affluent part of town. One hundred and fourteen was the middle floor of a three storied building, 112 was beneath and 116 above. It fronted on to the high street and had a garden area stretching behind where the dunny would have been.

This was a street of manual workers skilled in a variety of trades: linen weavers, printer, milliner, yarn weaver, carter, blacksmith, shoe maker, stone dresser, grocer, reed maker....usually the household would comprise the parents and children but some were widows with children and several households had a lodger. Often the front of the ground floor would be a shop premise and the back the living quarters. At this time John Storrier himself was working as a Master Flesher - a qualified butcher. Just when he attained the skills to earn this position of Master is unknown; perhaps he had worked as a flesher before marriage or had done some butchering while he was farming.

The flesh or meat market was held once a week "It was roofed and slated all round and open to the heavens in the centre. It had a wooden gate at one end, made large enough to admit a

---

[140] ibid p 380

cart. The Fleshers had stands all round facing the centre in which the purchasers stood, The stands were covered with cloths, and had a very clean and tidy appearance. The carcase hung behind the stall or stand, and when cut down, laid out on the stand."[141]

Water for the household had to be fetched from the hand pump down the street. Carrying water was a source of cash for the young lads of Forfar, or "loons" as they were known. It was also "the gathering place of all the goodwives of the locality, and the spirited scen of their gossip and their gaiety. And it was also the rallying point of all their husbands, who forgathered there when the day's darg was done, to smoke the pipe of peace, to turn over the topics of the hour , and to drink the very cold water that gushed into the "pan hole" with never ceasing flow."[142]

Water pump in East High Street. Photo: Angus Council

---

[141] Forfar Worthies, Alan Reid p 76
[142] ibid p 73

The never ceasing flow was an exaggeration. During the years Jane lived in Forfar the debate raged over whether to install gravity fed piped water from the Grampian mountains to replace the town wells. Those for the modernisation quoted the unreliability of the wells in dry seasons and, while some springs were of fairly good quality, others were "subject to organic percolations" and unhygienic. The sewerage system and piped water were brought in to Forfar in 1877-8, just after the Storrier family left.

The street lighting at this time was not brilliant. According to Alan Reid the old globes were "difficult to clean , because the oil and the smoke from the wick, after the first hour or two after being cleaned and dressed, obscured the glass and thus only served to make the darkness visible. They could not be cleaned and re-dressed every few hours." The lamp lighter "went round the lamps daily to dress the wicks and with supplies of oil; also to clean the globes, that is if the state of the weather permitted him to do so…..he now and then put the oily and smokey tow into his mouth , while he dressed the wick and filled the oil. In doing so, he would again soil the globe, which again brought the tow into requisition; and when he finished he would again put the tow into his mouth, Thenhis mouth, indeed his whole face became so black that he resembled the very devil…."[143]

At the end of the nineteenth century sanitary inspectors found some Forfar residences which were "bad enough in all conscience" but one particularly bad case had "a suffocating smell and a dense cloud of smoke….inside a well known character …was enjoying his dinner of skindies and dip…The

___

[143] Ibid p 76

house was in beastly condition. One corner served as a coal bunker, while another contained wood and other rubbish, the refuse of which strewed the floor. The bed, or rather remains of one strung ingeniously together, stood by the fireside a few inches from the ground, and over it were spread a number of filthy rages, which seemed to do service as bed clothing, The tiny window shed little light into the room, which for the most part was dark....the tenant attempted to explain away the terrible stench by remarking that her chimney was singularly difficult to keep clean.....

The Pend, Forfar Photo Angus Council, Cultural Sevices

Another dwelling visited by the Inspector found the "tenant boiling hayseed over an open fire, as a fattening and flavouring mixture for his horse, The passage led directly into the stable and, as were afterwards informed , it sometimes served as an open sewer into the street. The horse is taken up a small stair at the front door, and thought the passage to the stable. The interior of the house was in an abominable state, The dirt stained windows, not much bigger than ordinary sized skylights, admitted little light, and in such a confined and sickening atmosphere it seemed to us astonishing how people could live there. Pools of dirty water stood on the floor, while the fireplace resembled an ash pit. The housewife was in keeping with her surroundings, and did not look as if she was extravagant with the soap."[144]

These dwellings however appear to be exceptions rather than the rule for those living in Forfar. The Storrier abode appeared to have big windows and as their house juttted forward from the row, being the first one where the road narrowed they not only had windows onto the road frontage but could also get a view and light from a west facing window. From here they could see all the activities on market and fair days which took place on East High Street. *East High St photo: Angus Council*

On market days the street was full of bellowing cattle; for the annual fair day it was packed with activities such as swing chairs and roundabouts and everyone wore their best attire. Other celebrated days were Yuletide, Halloween, and Valentines. There was a circus that brought much excitement for families, and then for the men, cock fighting matches.

Previous page: Fair day in Forfar.. The cattle were still being driven in to East Street for market when the Storriers were living in 114.

Looking down the road on fair days from 114 East High street there would have been plenty of activity
Photo: Angus Council, Cultural Services

The roads in Forfar were spacious compared to those of

Kirriemuir and had many impressive red sandstone buildings. There had been areas, "jambs" where the through roads had narrowed but these had been widened to allow the galloping horses of the mail coaches to pass through. These mail coaches came through daily, one travelling north, the other south. The horses, it appears, were "overdriven....these poor animals, every time they arrived, were covered with sweat and foam and every muscle of their bodies quivered with fatigue - so rapidly were they driven."[145]

CASTLE STREET, FORFAR.   P. F. PATRICK, FORFAR,

Photo Angus Council, Cultural Services

In these early days the entire postal organisation was conducted in a small shop in East High Street; at one time a crabbed old body known as Postie Tamson did all the deliveries. A custom that complicated deliveries was the continued use of a woman's maiden name even after years of marriage. Thus one letter addressed to a Mrs Roberts of Forfar was undelivered as

[145] Shar'ly no' anither kirn Poke a' Forfar, Alan Reid p 82

no one of that name was known. The postman left the letter with a householder names Shusie Tam who promised to make faithful enquiries, only to remember a few days later that Roberts was indeed her own name by marriage but it was so long since she had used it that she had clean forgotten it!

For a family habituated to the countryside Forfar must have appeared to be all stone and cobbles. The streets though were lively; Alan Reid [146]remembers how there were "cripples and dummies" who were to be taunted or ignored by the young "loons"; when setting out to describe these street folk Reid "scarcely knows where to begin, for their number seems legion. Some were eccentric, some half-daft, some funny, some wild, some harmless, and all were well known to the loons of Forfar."

There were to sales folk in the street such as Herd, a smelly fish seller who, on being asked to move along by a constable, let off such a tirade that the constable went of "like a whipped cur"; there was Scud Moyes whose clothes were in tatters but who was used by another to augment his income, leading him out by the hand saying "ow he's puir daft- a'm juist takin' him t'e asylum" and thus wheedling ham and milk from housewives. Another merchant, Meg Fodd "sold small wares from a creel, and never marched from town without a big green cotton umbrella and with a very old-fashioned poke bonnet on her head. Meg had a curious bur to her voice and she hated the whole breed of boys who mimicked her..."

The two older Storrier children continued their schooling in Forfar. Elizabeth (fourteen) and John (twelve), together with their thirteen year old cousin Ann Robertson, were attending a

---

[146] Forfar's Worthies op cit, pp7-13

town school. That Elizabeth, John and Ann were still scholars in their early teens indicates that the family was not too badly off. Other young ones of similar ages who lived in East High street were already working; these teenagers had various employments, one a factory worker, another a draper's assistant; then there was a steam loom weaver and an apprentice printer.

Ann's mother Margaret was house keeping for her father at McRitch in Lintrathen. The two younger Storrier children however were sent back to Lintrathen to attend school there. The sisters, Jane and Margaret, had in effect swapped children, Ann to go and live with her Aunt Jane in Forfar while and Charles and James went to Lintrathen. Ten year old Charles was with his grandfather at McRitch while eight year old James stayed down the road at Ley with his father's unmarried sister Susan. Perhaps the comparative healthiness of life in the country was one of the reasons the two boys were kept in the countryside. They could continue their education there whilst also providing useful help on the farm to earn their keep. This was still a time when young children were often absent from school when they were required to help on the farm. In April of 1871 these two boys were listed as scholars in Lintrathen.[147]

Country School Days in the 1870's

While the older children were scholars in Forfar, the two younger boys were at Backwater school. Their teacher was Jane Anderson who lived with her mother Catherine. Jane was just twenty four and unmarried. Another young female teacher in a small country school, Isabella Murray, wrote a diary which well describes what these schools and their teachers were like.

---

[147] see 1871 census taken for Lintrathen area 02-04-1871

Isabella herself had left home aged eleven and when she was thirteen had gone to be a housekeeper and helper for her brother who was a Doctor in Glasgow. When she was eighteen she thought she "would go in to teacher's training so that I might do for myself, and a younger sister might take my place"[148]. Her brother and family had not encouraged her fearing that she would ruin her chances of marriage. She was not to be put off and joined a preparatory class doing a further two years study after which she did a teachers training course for which she had to walk four miles there and back and would often have to work until midnight or later to complete her studies.

On her arrival the outgoing teacher, who had been living at the school house with her mother, had little time to talk. She had mentioned that she wished Isabella to report a malicious boy to the Clerk of the School Board; as she was leaving she did not do it; his name was James Fraser. Reporting the boy would get him dismissed. There were forty children enrolled aged between five and fifteen and divided in to six classes.

On her first day the "children all mustered well and I soon discovered the boy who was to be reported to the Clerk to be dismissed. No sooner did he enter than, pulling a knotted cord out of his pocket, he whipped all the bare legs as he went to his seat. Soon there was a howling noise, and after silence was restored I opened the school with prayer and praise..........Jim

---

[148] Isabella Murray was sole Teacher at Kinlochewe from 1878. This from a transcript of her memoirs prepared by her great-granddaughter Kate Young held at Gairloch Museum.

Fraser was known as the worst boy in the whole place. He was brought up by his grandmother who had no control over him. He was over fourteen years old and could hardly read owing to his irregular attendance. He was a hard boy and was a most determined, self-willed boy and so became an object of prayer. He continued for a few days molesting the children and I took little notice of him, but a visitor arrived and I had to leave the school for a short time and it would be pandemonium.

"Calling James to my table, I confided in him and gave him a slate to write down the names of all who were making a noise in my absence and to see that they were all doing their work. He straightened himself up and looked his best and assured me he would do as I told him. I was detained longer than expected, but not a sound was heard and on my entering, James showed the slate with no names written. I thanked him for his services and told him to make up for lost time if he could. I had no more trouble with him afterwards. He came regularly to school, wrote his exercises carefully out - even more than I gave the rest of the class - and all the rest followed his example. He would come and delve the garden or sweep or dust the school as well as keep order in the playground. He no longer bullied the younger ones , but rather helped them.

"There was another boy younger than Jim, Donald Fraser, son of the leading elder. His parents were a little prejudiced against the young teacher and the boy had not the same respect for me as the others. However, I was enabled to gain it. Not many days after, the boys were playing in the field and Donald fell over the fence and put his arm out of joint. There was no doctor in the place nor within forty miles probably. I desired that this might be a means of blessing, and taking the boy to my house , I pulled his arm firmly and it gave a crack and went into its place. I then put it up in a sling and sent him home. The boy was relieved of pain and told his parents of the teacher's skill. Their prejudice was overcome and we became great friends. The fame of the operation spread over the glen so that the saying was common, "she looks like a child, but has the head of an old person.......

" I had two or three evening for the bigger girls who came to sew and knit, bringing also their darning and garments for repair. It was considered a great entertainment to assemble in my kitchen with a bright fire and lamp light, quite a contrast to their homes. The room was large and they sat round the table. The elder ones cut out garments, so helping their mothers. It was surprising to see the amount of work done in a few months and the parents were pleased. Someone read interesting stories so that two hours were spent very pleasantly and profitably. The boys were helping in the fields, but they had their own amusements during the play hours........". [149]

After 1876 inspectors went around the small Scottish schools to assess them. The following criticisms show what was expected: "This school is conducted with good order and discipline. The results on the whole pretty fair. Reading is fair throughout but must be more fluent and correct in the lower classes. Writing is very good. Arithmetic is the weakest feature in this school and demands the earnest care and attention of the Teacher. Singing is harsh and lifeless. The grant for the Infants will not be recommended in future unless more work is done by them. The teacher must throw more energy into his work, and must try to overcome the slovenly and inattentive habit noticeable among the children." [150]

---

[149] ibid pgs 6-8

[150] school log book at Gairloch museum dated May 2 1876 -August 23

Plans to Emigrate

The move into Forfar, like the shift to Carmylie, had been darkened for the Storrier family. On June 24 1870 their youngest child, David, died. He had convulsions for twelve hours and died in the early hours of the morning. He was six years old. Both his parents and a doctor were there. Whilst there was a tale carried down the generations that he had eaten too many green apples, his death was likely to have been caused by meningitis, although tetanus or epilepsy are other possibilities.

Whether the death of David was the catalyst for John to emigrate we do not know. Perhaps he had access to more news of opportunities in the colonies, or was not happy with town life in Forfar; he may even have come to Forfar in preparation for emigration. In 1872 the statistics showed how difficult it was to better oneself through farming for as John Mitchell[151] wrote "...it appears to me that the land tenure of Scotland is most unsatisfactory........Scotland, in fact, does not belong to the people of Scotland. They are permitted to reside in it, and practise their callings, but they appear to be merely tenants at will. Beyond the feu[152] of a house or villa, or the small space assigned as their last resting-place, few of the population can claim as property any part of their native soil.

"Although our kingdom contains upwards of three and a half

1895.
[151] Reminiscences of my life in the Highlands op cit p120
[152] "feu" - leasehold, feu-ing was the main method of leasing land in Scotland

million of inhabitants, who are supposed from their education to be the most
enlightened and intelligent people in Europe, yet they possess no interest in the territory of Scotland, One-half of their country is owned by seventy proprietors, while nine -tenths belongs to seventeen hundred persons....twelve proprietors own ...nearly a quarter of the whole of Scotland." [153] And the land owners according to Mitchell too often were not in a position to be good land lords to their farmer tenants: " ...these great Scotch estates seem unmanageable. With all the good qualities and talents of many of the proprietors, most of them appear helpless in regard to their pecuniary transactions.

"They are almost all in straitened circumstances, and consequently cannot do justice to the improvements of the country or the land they possess. Notwithstanding their great revenues, they are mainly dependent on their lawyers for the administration of their affairs. This is greatly owing to the extent of their estates, the law of primogeniture, and the fetters of entail and settlement."

It is not surprising that a hard working farmer such as John Storrier would be attracted to a country where it was possible to purchase his own property.

By June 1871 John was organised to leave Forfar. He was leaving his wife and family behind, it would be five years before they were reunited.

---

[153] Mitchell took these and other statistics from the 1872 Blue Book containing acres and rentals of the landed estates in Scotland.

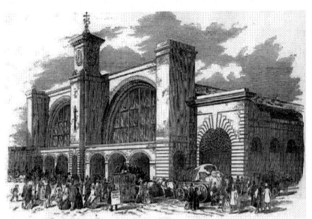

Kings Cross station from London Illustrated News 23 Oct 1852

Chapter 4

Leaving Scotland for the New World

"A magnificent lot of hardy pioneers....no wasters, no drunkards, no unemployable were to be found amongst them. This was the pleased opinion of a Queenslander on the arrival of a ship which the colonists had organised. The recruitment of people who would benefit the new Australasian colonies was a much debated topic. Men such as Henry Jordan, who arrived in London in 1861 as Emigration Commissioner , campaigned vigorously to persuade people to make the long journey to the new world. There were philanthropic groups who were keen to assist paupers to emigrate but these were not the type of people which men like Jordan were looking to recruit. He did not want "the sweepings" of British society. He was looking for industrious, virtuous and healthy folk, unashamedly sifting out any idiots, elderly or criminally inclined applicants.

Notices were posted in newspapers, handbills were published

and agents who had some experience of life abroad would be sent to market days to search out possible candidates. It was not that easy to up root agricultural labourers. There was still plenty of work on farms and employers were reluctant to let good workers go. And many of these people were deeply attached to the land they had lived and worked on for generations.

Robert Duncan, Jane's older brother, was one of those who was persuaded. In 1863, courtesy of the Queensland free passage policy on the Black Ball[154] shipping line, Robert and his wife Elizabeth left on the *Cairngorm*. They sailed from Greenock to Rockhampton and successfully settled[155] in Australia. Robert's occasional letters back to McRitch would arrive by a uniformed postman (with "pill box" hat), on a shore footed pony with a hogged mane, carried in a leather bag slung over the postman's shoulder. Charles Duncan paid the required postage when the letter arrived and everyone in the family including John and Jane would eagerly learn of the immigrants news.

Over a quarter of a million folk between 1860 and 1900 were to leave Britain for Australasia: "hope and optimism, stimulated by the possibility of becoming independent and self-sufficient , motivated many.... The new colon[ies] had land for the asking and, compared with "home" the wages were high".....and they had been led to believe that "they may find greater happiness and comfort there than they can attain in the country of their birth, where competition is so keen, where the strain of life is so severe and where the reward of labour seems

---

154 A very good description of the Black Ball line is given in Rights of Passage, Helen R. Woolcock
3 They settled in Coolarah, had 7 children, one of whom founded a very successful company RF Duncan & Co which is still in existence today "Livestock & Property Agents to Rockhampton

to them to be uncertain"[156]

Rather than go out together John went ahead with the idea of sending for his wife and family if the colonial life fulfilled the expectations built up by men such as Henry Jordan. There were earlier immigrants who had had bad experiences. One Frederick Tuckett on returning from New Zealand had been moved to write and distribute a booklet entitled –

DO NOT EMIGRATE
UNTIL YOU CAN POSSESS THAT PORTION OF THE LAND WHICH SHOULD BE YOURS: BEING A FEW REMARKS **ON THE SUFFERINGS OF EMIGRANTS IN SHIPS AND COLONIES ADDRESSED TO THE PEOPLE BY FREDERICK TUCKETT**[157]

Tuckett's first concern was for the welfare of female emigrants. These, he said, were suffering indignities due to the depravity of the crew, including the captains, mates, and Doctors. "Tyrannical, drunken, and in other respects sensual and depraved to a degree exceeding most other men, they exercise little self restraint; and having been subject to despotism, become despots in return, and are unfit to be entrusted with the power which, during a voyage, they generally abuse."[158] In fairness, he admits, "that impurity of conduct in emigrant vessels is also a reproach to the emigrants themselves, and furnishes strong ground to conclude that the reputation of our

---

156 Op cit p 25. These were remarks made by the Agent General for Queensland in 1871 but are equally applicable to those who travelled on assisted passages to New Zealand at this time.
157 First Published London 1850 reprinted by Frenchy Tuckett Society 2005
6   Do Not Emigrate Frederick Tuckett, 2005 p 4

country women for superior chastity is either a tradition of the past, or a mere fiction, the assertion of which is now libellous to the women of all other countries."[159] Further he says that for emigrants landed in New Zealand "dreadful orgies are the general rule, and not the exception."

His second criticism is the quality and quantity of food and water, the poor ventilation and the accommodation which was inadequate for health, comfort and decency. He goes on to say "But that which proves most fatal to peace and comfort in emigrant vessels, is intemperance, and the practice of using intoxicating drinks, whether to excess or not".[160]

And perhaps most damningly of all he criticized the publicity in Britain which he said was promoted by "land-jobbers" in London. These men were presenting an unrealistic picture of the land and the work available in New Zealand. "The islands of New Zealand are uncultivated wastes , either of mountains covered with dense forests, of plains and lowlands covered with high-ferned shrubs, or of swamps and marshes covered with rush and flax, without any open spots of grass land for pasturage, or of verdant downs and hills for sheep. In these vast tracts there is not to be seen a living animal, wild or domestic. Whatever is produced from the soil in New Zealand for the food of its population, either of grain from arable land, or of stock from pasturage, must be the work of time, by great labour and at much expense." An early explorer, Mr Brunner, is quoted - "I had previously seen the land from the coast, and thought it good and richly wooded, where, on inspection, I found a wet massy surface, with little, if any, vegetable soil." And in Tuckett's opinion "this is the error into which Captain

---

159 Ibid p5
8   ibid p6

Cook, and all others who have looked at New Zealand lazily from their ships or boats, without encountering the fatigues of an inspection have fallen; viz. The idea that the forests, beautiful and luxuriant to the eye as a landscape grow out of a rich and available land.

He advised people not to travel out to a colony unless those who had already arrived were proving their prosperity by remitting money back to the homeland. Letters appearing in newspapers extolling the fortunes of new immigrants to Australasia were often, he said, the fabrication of agents who made money out of recruitment. Often even when the immigrants had the means to write and send a letter they were never delivered as the recipients could not afford to pay the postal dues. The reality was that in 1850 while money was being made and remitted back from America, this was not the case of New Zealand. Twenty years later John Storrier decided to play it safe and go by himself rather than up rooting his whole family on an uncertain venture.

Fred Tuckett and others like him did not campaign in vain. Two years after his pamphlet was published Parliament passed legislation to protect emigrants rights on board ship and in 1855 it was amended to form the Passenger Act which remained in force for the following forty years. Officers in charge of seeing that the regulatory conditions for emigrants on board were implemented claimed that they were over worked and underpaid. Nevertheless the detailed legislation based on the firmly held Victorian faith that "all social improvements ...have their roots in cleanliness" greatly benefited the travellers of the second half of the nineteenth century. Organisers of the Black Ball line noted that "in contrast to the powerlessness of curative medicine, the power of preventing disease is about the happiest possession of science." The Passenger Act also reflected the new concept that a civilised government had a duty to "protect its subjects from insidious attacks of diseases...assaults of crime or from accidents."[161]

John Storrier had already broken his ties with the land having moved out of the Glens to Carmylie and then to town life in Forfar. His application and journey was carefully planned. He needed official forms sent in and approved. It included a certificate showing he was in good physical and mental health, not " apparently mutilated or deformed in person, nor afflicted with any disease calculated to shorten life, or to impair physical or mental energy...that he was vaccinated for small pox and was entirely free from every disease usually considered infectious or contagious" signed by a surgeon. He also needed   references from two respectable householders who were NOT Publicans or Dealers in Beer or Spirits stating that he was an honest, sober and industrious man of general good character; and another reference testifying that he had never been convicted or imprisoned for any crime...riot, assault or drunkenness., or had been a recipient of parish relief. The main obstacle was his age as he was actually fifty one and Government subsidized travel was restricted to men forty five and under. Fortunately for him birth certificates were not required until after 1872 and no one challenged him when he gave his age as forty five. Whilst the government paid for the ship journey they did not pay for the journey to the ships departure point, this was one of the measure which made it harder for "the sweepings of society" to make the voyage.

When John came to leave for New Zealand he was saying good bye to a large family: besides his thirty six year old wife and

---

161   Rights of Passage p 83

children and four children then aged fourteen, twelve, ten and eight three were his in-laws at McRitch and his own three sisters, two brothers and their families. Round the twenty third of June in 1871 John said his goodbyes and caught a train from Forfar. He would go through to Perth and then Stirling to get to Waverley station in Edinburgh, perhaps arriving the night before to ensure that he did not miss the London train. The Special Scotch Express(later to become known as The Flying Scotsman) left daily for London at ten in the morning and took ten and a half hours. Pulled by a famous Flyer, one of the fastest engines in Great Britain, with driving wheels eight foot one inch in diameter, it is described as being "amongst the most beautiful and graceful locomotive types this country has ever seen".[162]

PhotoJonathanPotter.
Www.steamtraingalleries.co.uk/pic_doncaster_003.html
John took a second class ticket which gave him a space in a compartment with a pair of benches, seating five persons each, rather close together, covered and backed with some cheap but durable material. Each compartment had its own door, there

---

162   Began on the East coast line in 1870

were no through corridors on these trains, nor were there toilets or dining cars. The train had a twenty minute stop at York where travellers ate a hasty lunch and a further brief stop of ten minutes at Newcastle for an equally hasty pee behind a decorated iron screen built on the platform for this purpose. Being June the temperature on board would have been fine, in winter this journey could be icy cold and dark. First class passengers had paraffin lamps and they would tip porters to bring them foot warmers – flat metal hot water containers . They had spacious wing-and-elbow seats with stuffing and springs, seating six persons to a compartment. There was no third class travel on what came to be known as The Flying Scotsman until November 1887, as it was thought that carrying third class passengers would reduce the profitability of the service to the owners.

John arrived in London at eight thirty on a summers evening, plenty of light to see this great bustling metropolis as he rode in a horse drawn cab from Kings Cross station to the Dock area to find himself an inn for the night. The next day he found his way to the East India Docks from where his ship the Glenmark was to leave. The grandiose stone gateway of the East India Docks was an impressive entrance to the wharves. Once inside there was a forest of masts, numerous vessels at the loading berths moored alongside short jetties at right angles to the main wharf. The bowsprits with jib booms rigged in protruded one after the other, each with a large notice hung over the bows bearing the name of the ship and its destination. The docks teemed with people, material and produce to be loaded.

The Glenmark photographed in Lytellton

Carpenters worked right up to the last fixing the temporary berths between decks for the assisted immigrants. This deck (which would be dismantled on arrival in New Zealand to provide more cargo space for the return voyage), had by law to give six foot head room. The deck was divided in three by well secured bulkheads: single men were placed aft in the foremost compartment, the married couples and their children under fourteen in the middle, and the single women in the stern. Two tiered berths were built in, the lower one six inches off the floor and removable for cleaning purposes, and the upper bunk at least thirty inches above - this did not leave enough room for sitting on one's bed. The beds were arranged athwart ship and there was three to nine inches between the berth and the side of the ship. There had to be space beside hatchways and privies although some ships were "wet" and smelly despite these regulations. Before boarding everything was scraped, disinfected and painted.

Emigrants were told to arrive in London a few days before departure to be interviewed and checked over before boarding the ship – they could be rejected at this late date if found to be unhealthy or deemed in some way unsuitable. They needed to purchase bedding and utensils for eating. Too much filth and too many lice had come aboard when passengers used to bring their own mattresses stuffed with old rags. They had to show too that they had brought suitable clothing as the voyage usually involved periods of intense heat and freezing cold.

Each ship had cargo as ballast to be loaded below, then there was a section for the passengers trunks (which they could get access to during the voyage). On this trip the Glenmark had the crew plus twenty three full paying cabin class passengers and one hundred and eighty eight assisted immigrants. Of the last group an unusually high proportion were single young women, sixty one in all - eighteen came from Ireland and there were nine sets of sisters – but it is remarkable how scattered the origins of these young women were and how adventurous these young housemaids and general servants were to be setting out alone on what was most likely a one way trip to a strange country. In the family compartment there were forty three persons, most young married couples with none or one or two very young children. [163] There were thirty- three single men with a predominance of farm labourers and ploughmen

---

163 In this respect it had been noted by Australian officials that large poor families should not be encouraged as they tended not to cope well on arrival and basically were more trouble than help to the young colonies.

under thirty years old, John Storrier being the only farmer and easily the most mature member! It was highly likely John was given a job as constable on board, a job given to one of the emigrants to help the Surgeon keep order on board among the emigrants. If carried out satisfactorily a constable earned a modest remuneration.

Food enough for one hundred and forty days was required to be taken on board. It included salt beef, pork, preserved meat, suet, butter, breadstuffs (biscuit, oatmeal, flour) dried peas, rice, potatoes, carrots, onions, coffee sugar, molasses; mixed pickles, mustard, salt, pepper and the all important lime juice. Alcohol was confined to the stores of the surgeon for medicinal purposes.....ale in particular was thought to be beneficial for pregnant women. Then there were the live animals – sheep, chicken- kept on deck until slaughtered for the table.

When all was stowed away the passengers were taken aboard and finally on the 29th of June 1871 the Glenmark slid from its berth as crowds on land waved to the departing vessel. "Never, perhaps, do Englishmen so thoroughly throw off their reserve as on the occasion of such a parting, and we doubt whether the varied forms of demonstrative grief shown here expressed are at all exaggerated" wrote a reporter commenting on a painting made at this time of an emigrant ship's leave taking.[164]

The steam tug took them down to Gravesend but on arrival at the channel they were delayed a week waiting for favourable winds and it was not until Friday 4 August that the Pilot left them off Torquay. James and Jessie Lorimer[165] were among the

164The Parting Cheer in National Maritime Museum Greenwich
165Www.teara.govt.nz/en/biographies/3113/1. Biography of Jessie and James daughter Margaret..

married couples between decks and her diary relates how sea sick they were and how they had never anticipated how awful that was. But five days later he wrote more positively "Cocks are crowing, dogs are barking, birds are singing, children crying, women chattering, men talking about old times and what they are going to do when they reach New Zealand, and some tell us they feel the fleas biting, just as they do in England."

A month later he reports "Wednesday 22nd September. Very rough. The wet is coming through the decks in all directions, caused by the motion of the ship. It dropped upon our beds. We have been canvassing the ceiling and wedging our boxes in the cabin...I feel very hungry and can eat anything ...Jane cannot get on as well.

Thursday 12th October. Wind aft. Making good running. Distance 273 miles. Thoroughly sea sick...want a change of diet...more room. Jane wants one of Richards cabbages, and I want a good beef steak.

Thursday 26th October. Fearful rough night. The chains and rope are breaking in all directions. The main portion of the rigging to the main mast gave way. Captain, mates and boatswain are giving orders in all directions. We were frightened up at one o'clock in the morning. Jane was ready to jump out of bed, - fearful rolling. I never wish to experience such again, when we put foot on land once more.

Monday 30th October. Not much sleep in the night. Jane waited up until 1 o'clock tending on the sick. So she went oretiring to rest and saw some portion of the Peninsula Heads, came down, woke me up, quite overjoyed. I got up and found the winds had shifted allowing us to steer clear of the heads . Could not sleep after four o'clock. The ship is all alive, fearful noise and bustle.

Some have changed their attire and thrown their beds overboard, ready for landing. At eight o'clock we were outside the harbour about three miles off. Be calmed. High cliffs from the Headland with ridge running down to the sea, with a hut or two dispersed. It looks like plots of vegetation growing around the hollows covered with brushwood. They set fire to some of it during the day and at night it is a good guide. The wind has sprung up again banishing all our hopes. We are further off the Littleton Harbour in the evening than morning. The old adage looks true here "Foreign hills are green. And when you are there, There is nothing to be seen." Jane's heart is in her shoes.

Such were the frustrations of arriving under sail. But on November the first ninety five days after leaving London and eighty eight days after they got under sail they arrived in Lyttleton. An immigration officer, J. Edwin March, came aboard to inspect the ship and found no reason to hold up the disembarkation. How frustrating it must have been for those on board ships which arrived with cases of measles, whooping cough, scarlettina or other infectious diseases. These folk had to endure further weeks of quarantine after their three month cooped up sojourn on the ship.

Edwin March was most complimentary on the conditions of the Glenmark and her passengers:
"...no sickness of any importance occurred during the voyage...every attention was paid to carry out those sanitary measures laid down in the instructions issued by the Canterbury Government....I learned from the Immigrants in each compartment that the provisions had been served out in accordance with the dietary scale ....the Distilling Apparatus, under the charge of a skilful Engineer worked admirably throughout the voyage, and the supply of water was abundant.

194

..."[166] accordingly March recommended the payment of all gratuities and the further employment of the Surgeon-Superintendent. The Surgeon's on these ships were in charge of the emigrants and under him was a Matron in charge of the women on board, whilst Constables from among the passengers were paid a small gratuities for assisting in keeping order. Surgeons and matrons and the emigrants themselves varied in character from ship to ship and John was obviously fortunate in the Glenmark.

The official log for the journey recorded that the vessel passed through large fields of ice for several days, the officers having an anxious time....which must have been the occasion of the Lorimer's sea sickness and fear in the latter part of the trip.

John soon obtained employment in New Zealand yet it was five years before he sent for Jane and his children. Was he making very sure that they had a good future in Canterbury or did it take that time for him to accumulate the money to provide a home for them? Or was it that he had to work that long to get a New Zealander to nominate his family for emigration? These are unanswered questions. What did happen was that John worked for a prominent member of the New Zealand Parliament's upper house, William Robinson. He worked on Mr Robinson's large estate in North Canterbury, "Cheviot Hills" as a ploughman for the next five years. He was earning £1 a week and we do not know if he remitted some of this to Jane in Scotland or whether he saved what he did not need for the farm they later bought at Ealing out of Christchurch.

---

166 Commissioner's Report-Ship Glenmark
Genealogy.rootweb.ancestry.com

Jane and the children follow their father to New Zealand

It is not known how Jane supported herself and her children during the five years after her husband sailed for New Zealand. She may have had a job, or John could have remitted some of his wages, or her father could have assisted. When Jane's father died in 1890 Jane was left £50 compared to the £150 her other two sisters received, suggesting either less need or that she had already had help. Whatever the situation John did not send for his family until he had obtained subsidised fares for them.

By 1876 Mr Robinson had agreed to nominate Jane and the four children for assisted emigration to New Zealand. Ship passage payments were made to emigrants selected by UK agents as John had been, or they could be given to Europeans who had New Zealand residents who were prepared to nominate them. The scheme had been set up in 1869 when the New Zealand government borrowed ten million pounds to get public works under way (including roads and railways) and there was a dire need for a work force.

Five years after John had left it was the turn of Jane and her children to go to McRitch and bid their farewells. Jane's father took them all to the smart stone built station at Kirriemuir. It must have been a great adventure for them all: Jane now a healthy forty one year old who had been working as a house keeper and her grown children, Elizabeth eighteen years old and trained as a house servant and the boys John, seventeen, Charles sixteen and James fourteen, all well able to look after themselves. The train ambled through countryside until Kirriemuir Junction, which had no road access and was merely a couple of low platforms. Here they transferred to the train for

Perth and then on, as John had done to Edinburgh, for the train to London.

Jane must have been thankful to have strong children to help with the luggage as they negotiated the platforms, especially at Waverley station in Edinburgh where in summer there was " a scene of confusion so chaotic that a sober description of it is incredible to those who have not themselves survived it. Trains of caravan length come in portentously late from Perth, so that each is mistaken for its successor; these have to be broken up and re-made on insufficient sidings, while bewildered crowds of tourists sway up and down amongst equally bewildered porters on the narrow village platform reserved for these most important expresses; the higher officials stand lost in subtle thought, returning now and then to repeated inquiries some masterpieces of reply couched in the cautious conditional, while the hands of the clock with a humorous air survey the abandoned sight till at length, without any obvious reason and with sudden stealth, the shame stricken driver hurries his packed passenger off..." [167] Waverley station was made from three different railway companies each of which began with their own terminus and when they united to form Waverley it was said to be with such imperfect results that it became unsurpassed in the nineteenth century for its inconvenience.

They would have found their train without too much difficulty with its distinctive livery of varnished teak and gold lettering with red shading. Earlier in the year there had been a terrible

---

167 Described by Foxwell in 1889, The Railways of Britain, Jack Simmons, pg219-10

accident on this line with the Scotch Express[168] colliding with a coal train at Abbots Ripton. Fourteen people had been killed and as a result the signalling systems and the emergency braking mechanisms on the carriages had been revised. There were dangers associated with this new speedy travel " The public will travel as fast as they an. The Railway Companies will supply the highest speed they can ...It does not even appear that the quick recurrence of disasters and the large aggregate of fatalities have much effect in dampening the general eagerness to get ahead in the hurry-scurry of modern life" wrote one reporter that summer of 1876.[169]

The journey had not changed significantly since John made it five years earlier although the luggage which previously was stowed away in an overhead shelf in the carriage was now placed in one of the luggage brakes at the rear of the train. Still no toilets or dining cars so just the one opportunity at York to have time off the train; stops for the steam engine's water supply being considered too short and there being this Victorian obsession for getting the trains to their destinations exactly on time and as efficiently as possible. Most likely Jane had a picnic basket as the meal which could be ordered at York was two shillings and sixpence – it consisted o of "Soup, Joints, Vegetables, Tart & Cheese, with Warning given in the rooms FIVE MINUTES BEFORE the train departure."
Arriving at the impressive Kings Cross station built in 1850 their Scottish taste possibly preferred the functional simplicity of the architecture compared to the very ornate St Pancreas

---

168 This train did not officially have its famous name of The Flying
Scotsman until 1923. The Special Scotch Express first left Kings Cross and
Edinburgh
simultaneously in 1862 and apart from a short period during World War 1
there were uninterrupted departures at this time for the next 125 years.
169 London Times Aug 29 1876

station alongside. Kings Cross was also the market station where produce including animals arrived from the countryside. So outside was a crowd of people, horse drawn cabs and drays for food stuffs. Jane and the family needed to get to the southern basin of the West India Docks. It is quite a distance across London, an option was to get horse drawn transport for themselves and their trunks to the Thames and then a small taxi row boat east along the river to the West India Dock.

Before embarkation Jane and the family would have had another health inspection. These were not always comprehensive, such was the bustle of departure and the work load of the inspectors. There were other problems such as the measles epidemic that had recently been flourishing in the Docks. Once on board there was a problem as their berths. Their ticket which had been arranged from New Zealand, was for a family in the middle compartment. But as the boys were seventeen, sixteen and fourteen years they were deemed to be too old for the family area and were transferred to the single men's quarters.

Entrance to West India Docks (portcities.co.uk)

The Waitangi was a slightly larger ship than the Glenmark being 1128 tons compared to 958. It was owned by the New Zealand Shipping Company set up by Christchurch men for bringing emigrants and exporting goods, especially farm produce. It was advertised as being "of the highest class....their saloons are fitted with all the latest improvements to ensure the comfort of the passengers, and the tables are supplied on a most liberal scale." Admittedly this was aimed at the full fare paying passengers but having only been built two years previously it was deemed to be a good ship to be booked on. It was owned by the New Zealand Shipping Company set up by Christchurch men for bringing emigrants and exporting goods, especially farm produce.

The day they left there was a huge fire further up river at Brooks wharf. The smoke was visible from the West India Docks and floating fire fighting boats were sent to extinguish the blaze. The family wanted to stay on deck as the Waitangi was towed by a tug out of the docks and down river to Gravesend. The deck was a busy and cluttered area – toilets, cook houses, animals, rigging, wheelhouse machinery, life boats as well as distilling apparatus. Single men and families were allocated separate areas on the main deck which they could use whenever they liked. (Single women could use the poop along with the saloon passengers, though only at specified times, their life being more strictly monitored for their own protection, even to having iron bars to the hatchway to their sleeping quarters.)

At Gravesend some more paying saloon passengers came aboard then the tug took them down to Beachy Head and out in to the Channel where a fair wind was blowing and they had their last sight of the white cliffs of England. For many adjustment to life on board meant getting over sea sickness, a complaint that defied all attempts to understand or prevent – many hypothesis were put forward from too much or too little blood to the brain or spinal cord, others thought constitutional or psychological factors might be involved as it was noted that some passengers of strong physical make up and some with "strong heads" were not so affected by sea sickness.
One Waitangi passenger described the daily food program:
" ...rise in the morning at &. Breakfast at 8 o'clock Dinner at 1 Tea at 5. We have as many hard biscuits as we like but they don't suit anyone that have got bad teeth because they are so

very hard."[170]

Montage of sketches depicting life on board an immigrant ship showing emigrants embarking at the London docks, scrubbing the decks, watching a passing ship, dealing with heavy seas, catching an albatross, and queuing at the surgery. Taken from The Illustrated New Zealand Herald 9 April, 1875 www.nzhistory.net.nz

---

170 Www. pycroft.co.nz from transcript of his ancestors Waitangi voyage diary

There was some variation on the standard of the food partly due to how good a cook you had assigned to your section. The cooking and cleaning was rostered among the emigrants. The voyage was for many the biggest holiday they had ever experienced. Women cleaned, prepared meals, exercised, did needlework, and chatted. The young men were sometimes bored but there were free libraries and a variety of amusements according to the talents of those aboard – plays, dances, concerts, sometimes a fiddler, even brass bands; athletics, quoits and other physical game were organised by the passengers. And then there were the religious services on Sundays. These were sometimes abandoned due to sectarian differences and frequently suffered from poor attendance, although at other times were attended by those with little faith as something to do.

The Storrier family were fortunate, there were no major storms or calms and the trip was made in the good time of eighty eight days from London to Lyttelton. The family reunited, after five years, moved into Hanmer Street, Avonvale in Christchurch. They lived here for ten years before moving to a farm in Ealing. Later they would move to Timaru where their eldest son John had set up a business known as the Timaru Foundry. John and Jane lived to see the foundry grow in to a flourishing engineering business. None of the emigrant Storrier family ever returned to Scotland and by the time their descendants made the return voyage in the mid twentieth century John and Jane's world had gone...McRitch was covered by a lake formed by a dam to provide water for Dundee and the hills behind were covered in foreign pine. The immigrants numerous descendants did well in the new country and by the twenty first century considered themselves New Zealanders, never thinking as their grandparents had done that "home" was Scotland.

Landing immigrants at Lyttelton, NZ. A busy dock scene with steam and sailing ships, wharf buildings, and families awaiting their luggage, collecting their luggage and greeting friends and relations. Some are still being helped off the ship onto the wharf. From Illustrated Australian News, 16 January 1878

EPILOGUE

The connection which kept the Scottish and New Zealand families in touch.

The Scot abroad, though seas divide
Still wafts his thoughts to home
Not spreading leagues nor rolling tide
Can bind the exile's heart to hide
To rest and yet to roam.

The pride is to be Scotland's bairn
Tho' banished from her breast
Tho' of her soil, hill, strath and glen
She spared no foothold's space,
She breathed the birthright of her men,
And bade his brave heart win again
The battle of his race. [171]

Missives from the colonies would have been delivered by horseback to the family left behind: a postman in Angus 1870's

John and Jane Storrier never returned to Scotland after they left in the 1870s. Handed down in the New Zealand family were

---

[171] Hills of Home p154.

photographs which had been sent to Jane from her father, Charles Duncan. We do not know how much John corresponded with his family back in Scotland but we do know that contact was kept between John's descendants in the colony and the descendants of his brother, William Storrier in Scotland.

In the middle of the twentieth century John's great grandchildren had the opportunity to return to what had always been referred to as "the home country". By then the only relatives they knew of in Scotland were the Storrier family, Susan, William, James and David. It was Jane and John's great granddaughter Jean Storrier Skinner who first returned to Scotland. Her mother's sister, also called Jean Storrier in New Zealand, had an address in the parish of Lintrathen where she had written postcards to "Cousin Susan Storrier, Burnside Cottage, Ballintore. The younger Jean Storrier Skinner duly met Susan and two of her brothers, David and James. She also met the son of the third brother, William who it transpired had in his possession postcards sent by Jean Storrier from Timaru in 1907.

"Father wrote your father a letter", wrote sixteen year old Jean Storrier from New Zealand in 1907. Her card was to "Dear Cousin Susan" who was living in the cottage, Burnside of Ballintore, in Lintrathen. Susan was twenty four at this time but she kept these cards until she died aged one hundred and two in 1986. "Do you collect postcards?" her young relative Jean had eagerly enquired, and while the first card was formerly signed "from Jean D. Storrier" the later ones were sent "with best love and kisses, Jean Storrier."

The two fathers referred to in these postcards were James Milne Storrier in Scotland and James Duncan Storrier in New

Zealand. As boys both had spent time in Lintrathen, but as James Milne Storrier was fifteen years older than his namesake cousin and went to work in Glen Shee as a young shepherd it is uncertain whether they ever met in person.

It was their fathers, John and William Storrier who must have had a close friendship. John, who emigrated, had three brothers none of whom had legitimate sons. There was Charles the oldest boy who was a cattle dealer in Glenisla. Although living until he was 76 he had not married until he was 46 and his wife Ann McNicoll was 42 years old when they married and they had no children.

There was Andrew, the youngest, who also lived until he was 76 who remained a bachelor living in Angus all his life as a shepherd.

Then there was William, two years older than John. In 1847 William was 29 and John 27, grown men but unmarried. Farming near to the Storriers in Lintrathen had been the Milne family. This family worked a farm of 45 acres which employed four men. The oldest daughter was Betty also known as Betsy. In 1847 Betsy gave birth to a son, James, and William Storrier was named as the father. Betsy was 28 and William 26 when their son was born.

Betty, or Betsy, had a brother James who farmed at Cauldcots in the Fettercain parish. Their mother who had been widowed was living with at Cauldcots and it was here that the unmarried Betsy came for the birth of young James. He was baptised as James Milne Storrier in 1847 in the Fettercain Parish. In 1848 his mother Betsy married another man, a miller named John Grant. This couple had six children and at some point the young James Milne Storrier went to live with his paternal grandmother Storrier in Lintrathen.

William meanwhile worked on his uncle's farm at Tannadice

but later moved back to live with his widowed mother and work as a shepherd in Lintrathen. Also in this household is this thirteen year old son James. William then had an influence on the upbringing of his son James and no doubt spoke of his brother John who had taken his family to live in New Zealand.

One evening in early spring of 1862 William died of convulsions. On his death certificate his brother Charles testified that William had suffered from these convulsions for years which perhaps explains his early death aged forty three and why he and Betsy had never married. He left a healthy son living there at Ley with his grandmother Janet McKenzie Storrier. Three years after his father's death James' grandmother also died. By this time James was a young man of 16 years and he left to work as a shepherd at Glen Shee, still in Angus but further north.

James Milne Storrier' s birth was recorded in the Fettercain church registry as being the "natural" son of William Storrier. It is from this natural son that the most illustrious Storrier family members came. James Milne Storrier was to live a long life. In 1941 the Kirriemuir Free Press reported "Death of Lintrathen Crofter. The death occurred at a Dundee nursing home last weekend of Mr James Storrier, Burnside, Lintrathen, in his 94th year. A native of the Fettercain district, Mr Storrier before residing in the Lintrathen district, was for a number of years a shepherd in the Glenshee area, and took over the croft at Burnside, Lintrathen, more than 40 years ago. He was predeceased by his wife (Ann Stewart Robinson) about nine years ago, and is survived by three sons and a daughter. Two of his sons, James and David, are police Superintendents in the respective cities of Glasgow and London, both being attached

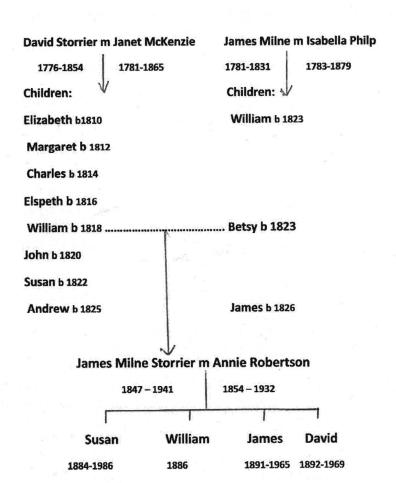

David Storrier m Janet McKenzie   James Milne m Isabella Philp

1776-1854   1781-1865   1781-1831   1783-1879

Children: Children:

Elizabeth b1810   William b 1823

Margaret b 1812

Charles b 1814

Elspeth b 1816

William b 1818 .... Betsy b 1823

John b 1820

Susan b 1822

Andrew b 1825   James b 1826

James Milne Storrier m Annie Robertson

1847 – 1941   1854 – 1932

Susan   William   James   David

1884-1986   1886   1891-1965   1892-1969

to the division. David, it will be remembered, was for a number of years acting as bodyguard to the Duke of Windsor."

James Milne Storrier and his wife Ann had four children. Their oldest, Susan, known in New Zealand as Cousin Susan, never married. It was Susan who carried on the correspondence with her New Zealand relatives, sending post cards to her second cousin Jean Duncan Storrier who lived in Timaru. Susan lived until she was 102, and over ninety of these years was spent in the home she was born in, Burnside of Balintore in Lintrathen. It was at Burnside that her young second cousin twice removed, Sandra, from New Zealand visited her. This was in 1963 when Susan was nearly eighty. Sandra found herself in cottage belonging to a bygone era, small, dark, cold and with very little furniture. A scarcity of amenities that she had not come across in her colonial life.

Susan's younger brothers were William, James and David. William was a successful Glasgow business man (seller of soft drinks). It was James and David that the New Zealand relatives met in the 1950's. On his death in 1965 James was described by the Kirriemuir Free Press as follows: "....a native of Burnside Ballintore, Lintrathen, he retired to Kirriemuir after an illustrious career with the Glasgow Police Force. Superintendent of the marine division, he held the post of Assistant Chief Constable on his retirement. A member of the Kirriemuir Town council, he served terms a junior and senior magistrate and latterly as Police Judge. Mr Storrier was a keen golfer. He is survived by his wife, sister and brothers....."

James' brother David was 77 when he died and many obituaries were published, amongst them the following in the Kirriemuir Free Press: "....Superintendent Storrier was educated at Websters seminary, Kirriemuir and later in Dundee. He was a school teacher in Glasgow before joining the Metropolitan Police. For 18 years he shadowed the Duke of Windsor, as Prince of Wales, King and ex-King, accompanied him to exile. When the Duke of Windsor renounced the throne, Mr Storrier accompanied him aboard the destroyer that took him to exile. And became the only official link between the Duke and his former Kingdom. He was present at the Duke's wedding and continued his duties as guardian Shadow in Austria, Italy, Czechoslovakia, and France. It was the superintendent's responsibility to secure privacy for the Duke and to discourage curious sight seekers. He remained with the Duke for two years after his abdication before returning to the Metropolitan Police. He became Superintendent of an east end division, then took over A division the most important in the area, which included the royal Palaces, Houses of Parliament, Whitehall and Downing Street. Superintendent Storrier retired from the police service in 1948. At the time of his retirement he was the most decorated police officer in Britain. He was awarded the MBE and MVO as well as numerous foreign decorations........."

Jean Hay writes "...when I first met David in London in 1953, he was involved in some sort of Secret Service, so he had not actually retired as suggested...when I first called the landlady didn't want to tell me if indeed David lived there until I explained that I was a relative. She also didn't know where David worked but told me that he was picked up each morning and the car could go in any direction. He was still working for the Secret Service when Jean and Geoff Parsons visited him a few years later." Given the outstanding careers of David and James it was a curiosity that when Jean Hay met Cousin Susan in Scotland she, like her brothers did with Jean and Geoff, said that the Duncan's were the interesting family members who should be looked up.

"The Duncan family were well-born" said Cousin David Storrier to Granma Jean in 1956 when they met in London. David knew of his grandfather's brother, John, who had married Jane and who later had his wife and children brought out to New Zealand. Cousin David, when he spoke of the Duncan's being well-born was referring to this Jane whose parents were Charles Duncan and Margaret Farquharson. Why should David have made this remark when both the Duncan and Storrier family had come from similar backgrounds in Glenisla? Furthermore it was a sentiment expressed again by David's brother James when he met his New Zealand relatives (Granma Jean and Geoff) and took them to Kirriemuir to visit the house where James Barrie had lived. (Barrie had died nearly twenty years previously but his housekeeper lived on in his home on Brechin road and it was she who showed Jean and Geoff around).

This could be due to the strong character and achievements of Charles Duncan as until Charles came along there seems to be little to differentiate between the Duncan and the Storrier families. They were both families of long standin in Glen Isla and Lintrathen who worked on the land although they did not own any land themselves. Charles married into the Farquharson family who could trace back a long lineage. Then he became a land owner considerably better off than small crofters or landless agricultural labourers. His final home in East Campsie was a substantial two storied stone building with a high stud and large windows. It was an unusual house for its time being built more in the fashion of a small mansion than a regular farmer's dwelling. He and his son who lived with him are photographed in front of this house wearing kilts. By this time the kilt would have been worn not as a result of tradition but of fashion, a fashion which had taken off among the well to do following Queen Victoria's love for the tartan . Charles had about him the air of a successful man and this is the impression that he left with his Storrier nephews and nieces, connected to him by his daughter Jane's marriage to John Storrier.

In 1956, eighty years after Jane Duncan left Scotland forever, Granma Jean and Geoff arrived at the farm where Jean's great grandmother Jane Duncan had been born.

Photo: Jean Parsons

The valley that summer of 1956 was a spacious fertile area, with rich grass for the black beef cattle. The farmlands had changed since Jane had left, emptier, with fewer people and buildings and without the variation in land use. [172] There were

---

[172] This valley was subsequently flooded to form a water reservoir for Dundee

two houses and several outbuildings, the main dwelling then, while re roofed still retained its rectangular shape, small windows and central front door. It was two story building although the stud was not high, and the upstairs rooms must have been constricted in space as they are tucked under the sloping eaves with no gables. This may not however have been the home Jane was raised in as it was said that the main dwelling was consumed by fire early in the twentieth century.

What kind of land did Jane and her family imagine she was going out to? On leaving she took with her a silver locket with the photo of herself and her mother inside. The outside was a simple pattern depicting a dove and a single tropical looking palm tree. It was common in those days to refer to the tropical climes of New Zealand, which, while real enough in the far north were not so accurate of where Jane was to live.

When the New Zealand descendants returned to Scotland in the mid twentieth century they had little to go on to find their Scottish relatives. The photos and the locket being the tangible links and the names of the Storrier cousins which had been told to them by their parents and grandparents. William and Betsy's story was not known then and it had been something of a mystery as to why the names of the Milne family had been written in a Storrier family bible alongside those of the Storrier's. And it was not until the tale of the natural son of William was discovered that the New Zealand family knew exactly how they were related to their Scottish Storrier "cousins".

A photo sent out Jane in New Zealand about 1885 with Charles Duncan in front the house he moved to at East Campsie. This, the "farm and shootings" were rented from the Airlie estate. Also pictured are his son James and his wife Ann [Robertson] and their two children Alexander and James. Still living at McRitch was Jane's other brother Charles and her sister Margaret.

Granma Jean who kept alive our Scottish heritage.

When we were children our mother Jean talked, especially at dinner time and seemingly endlessly, about our ancestors. She wanted us to "know" but her tales were hard to remember and since she had told them so often, it seemed impolite to ask too many questions. Besides when one did, the answers were often difficult to comprehend. From her dinner monologues we learned of our Scottish ancestors. It was impressed upon us that our heritage was "to learn to suffer" (Duncan clan motto) and to have "faith and fortitude" (Farquharson clan motto). Way back in our lineage we learnt were connections to Robert the Bruce who, defeated and on the run, hid in a Highland cave and watched a spider spin a web over the doorway: six times the spider tried and failed, the seventh the spider succeeded. This, coupled with the little red engine who thought he could and thought he could and did it.....meant our family should/ could persevere when faced with difficulty. This seems to be a common theme in Scotland; the Ogilvy (our ancestors' landlords) motto is "to the end".

Mum had a table of connections in her head, similar to the biblical begat series, but it was so hard to remember the names. She had no access to records that the current genealogical interest has opened up today, Parish registers for example were outside her reach. History books of her generation focused on English political matters and the literature that was likely to come her way was about the upper classes. Now that was something she could and did look up, the Burkes Peerage records in London. Naturally her findings turned up the aristocrats for which she would find links in names and appearances. (So our brother Bill was linked to General Lee whose statue Mum saw in a visit to Washington DC).

We were left with an undefined sense of what it meant to have Scottish blood in our veins, and, according to Granma Jean, Royal blood at that. In my mind it was a people that lived in a craggy mountainous region, a people of high principles, mauve heather on the foothills, colourful tartans, misty lands, hard work and a cold climate. The Stone of Scone, Margaret Queen of the Scots, Rob Roy and Sir Walter Scot all featured in Mum's tales. We went to a Presbyterian school which was divided up in to Scottish Houses: Glamis, Loch Leven, Berwick, Stirling and Braemar. We belonged to Glamis, which as it turns out was not so far from our ancestors' homes in Glenisla and Lintrathen.

The connection to royalty for our family proved elusive to the genealogist descendants, Jean Hay and Bill Parsons. However recently, with the aid of ever more sophisticated computer software, a line has gone back all the way to Robert the Bruce. Curiously though, it came through our father's family who had left Scotland in the 16th century.. *Below: Jean Parsons 1914 - 1994*

BIBLIOGRAPHY

Angus Council Cultural Services, Forfar

Brett, Henry Sir *White Wings* Auckland 1924

Burt, Edward *Letters from a Gentleman in the North of Scotland* London 1822 (available on-line)

Chisom, Rev W D *Journey Down the Ages* 1983

Cockburn, Lord, *Memorials of His Time* Edinburgh 1946

Colman, Russel & Dennison E.P. *Historic Forfar the Scottish Burg Survey* Edinburgh 2000

Crighton, Marty *Poems* Dundee 1872

Cunningham Graham *A Century of Scottish People*

Devine T.M. The *Scottish Nation 1700-2007*, London 2006

Dobson David *The Jacobites of Angus 1689-1746 Part 1 and Part 2* USA 2009

Dormandy, Thomas *The White Death, A History of Tuberculosis* 1999

Duff David ed *Queen Victoria's Highland Journal* 1980

Fraser, Amy Stewart *Hills of Home* London 1973

Gibson, Rob *The Highland Clearances Trail* Edin. 2007

Grewer, David *The Story of Glenisla* Aberdeen 1926

Grey Graham, Henry, *Scottish Men of Letters* 1901

Hall John A *A History of the Peninsula War*

Hardy, John *Lintrathen and Glenisla*

Hay, Jean *A Highland Heritage, The Farquharson Clan* pvte publ. NZ 2008

Hogg, James *A Tour of the Highlands in 1803* Edinburgh 1986

Hudson W H (1841-1922 *A Shepherd's Life* London1981

Jackson, Lynda *The Milne Family* pvte publ. 2002Canada

London, Jack *The Railways of Britain*

McNeill F.M. *The Silver Bough Scottish Flk Lore and Folk Belief* Edin 1989

Mitchell, Joseph *Reminiscences of my life in the Highlands* Gt

Britain 1971 (orig. publ.1884)

Oman Sir Charles *A History of the Peninsula War* 1902

Ramsay, Dean *Reminiscences of Scottish Life and Character* Edinburgh & London abt 1872

Reid, Alan , *Forfar's Worthies and Incidents Fifty Years Ago,* Forfar 1912

Reid, Alan *The Royal Burgh of Forfar* London 1902

Roughead William *Twelve Scots Trials* 1913

Simmons Jack *The Railways of Britain* 1990

Smith, Adam *An Inquiry into the Nature and Causes of the Wealth of Nations* London 1910

Smith, James *Memoirs of James Smith Stonemason Dundee 1805-1869* www.scan.org.uk

Smout, T.C. *A History of the Scottish People 1560 -1830*, Fontana Press Gt Britain 1998

Smout, T. C. and Wood, Sydney *Scottish Voices 1745-1960*, Fontana Press 1991

Stewart, Katherine *Crofts and Crofting* Edin 2005

Stewart Fraser Amy *Hills of Home*

Sword Jessie *They did Wrong* 2005

Symon J.A. *Scottish Farming Past and Present* 1959

Turnock, David *The Historical Geography of Scotland since 1707* Cambridge 1982

Mann, Ernst Simpson *Shairly No' Anither Kirn Pokr o' |Forfar* Forfar and District Hist Soc

McKenzie, Dr John ed. Christina Byan Shaw *Pigeon Holes of Memory* Gt Brit 1988

McKenzie, Osgood Hanbury *A Hundred Years in the Highlands* paperback 1995

Mitchell, Joseph *Reminiscences of my Life in the Highlands vol 2(1884)* Gt Britain 1971

Murray, Isabella ed. Young, Kate School Teacher at *Kinlochewe Feb-Sep 1878 – her own account taken from her memoirs* by her great grand daughter. Unpubl. In Gairloch

museum see Kate@youngresourses.co.uk
Parsons, Bill *Jill Tompkins-Bailey, pt 1 & 2, a genealogical study* pvte publ. NZ 2008
Warden, A.J. *Angus or Forfarshire* vol XlV Dundee 1880
Whately Cristopher A *Scottish Society 1707 – 1803* USA 2000
Woolcock, Helen R *Rights of Passage Emigration to Australia in the 19thc* London 1986

MUSEUM
Angus Folk Museum, Kirkwynd, Glamis, Forfar

WEBSITES
Dsl.ac.uk (dictionary scots language)
Electricscotland.com
Genealogy.rootweb.ancestry.com
Portcities.co.uk
Pycroft.co.nz
Scotlandspeople.gov.uk
Tera.gov.nz
Undiscoveredscotland.co.uk

ABOUT THE AUTHOR
Jill Tompkins Bailey nee Parsons is the great great grand daughter of the Scottish emigrants John and Jane Storrier. Born in Wellington (1947) and studied history at Victoria University and later Cambridge University in UK. Married (1) Bruce Tompkins (1947-1992) , they had 4 children and lived in New Plymouth NZ; in 2004 married (2)A.J. Bill Bailey and now lives in Berkswell, U.K.